KIDS IN SPORTS

Shaping a Child's Character From the Sidelines

Bill Perkins
with
Rod Cooper, Ph.D.

MULTNOMAH

PORTLAND, OREGON 97266

To our wives,
Cindy Perkins and **Nancy Cooper,**
for their understanding and love.

And to our parents,
Lynn and **Francis Perkins** and **Avanell Cooper.**
Throughout our lives, they have shaped our character
from the sidelines.

Unless otherwise marked, all Scripture references are from the Holy Bible: New International Version, copyright 1973, 1978, 1984 by the International Bible Society. Used by permission of Zondervan Bible Publishers.

The Living Bible, copyright 1971 by Tyndale House Publishers, Wheaton, Il.

Cover Photo by Kevin Haislip
Author photos by Raleigh

KIDS IN SPORTS
© 1989 by Bill Perkins with Rod Cooper, Ph.D.
Published by Multnomah Press
Portland, Oregon 97266

Multnomah Press is a ministry of Multnomah School of the Bible, 8435 N.E. Glisan Street, Portland, Oregon 97220

Printed in the United States of America

Library of Congress Cataloging-in-Publication Data

Perkins, Bill, 1949-
        Kids in sports: Shaping a child's character from the sidelines /
by Bill Perkins and Rod Cooper.
        Includes bibliographies.
        ISBN 0-88070-229-X
        1. Sports for children—Psychological aspects. 2. Coaching (Athletics) 3. Personality development. I. Cooper, Rod. 1953- II. Title.
GV709.2P47   1989
796'.10'92201—dc19   89-3038
                                                                                          CIP

89   90   91   92   93   94   95   96   97   98   -   10   9   8   7   6   5   4   3   2   1

CONTENTS

FOREWORD

The best coaches I've ever played for were the ones who knew themselves and their players. Those exceptional coaches adapted their coaching style to the personality of each player and, ultimately, they were able to draw the best out of each player.

Even if my kids never become professional athletes or even good at athletics, I want them to enjoy playing sports. I'd like to be the kind of parent and coach who helps them learn to play the game of life, and makes them feel special doing it. Children's sports are a great place for young people to develop body coordination, self-esteem, teamwork, and mature personalities. But they need parents and coaches to help them learn more from sports than how to hit a baseball, throw a pass, or kick a soccer ball.

I know my parents cared much more for me as a person than an athlete when I was going through those difficult adolescent years. And I will never forget their time and effort in making me feel special and successful at such an early age.

In *Kids in Sports*, Bill Perkins and Rod Cooper provide the insight needed to aid parents in better understanding their children, to help them grow personally while competing in sports. I'm glad they wrote the book and know it will prove a priceless tool for both parents and coaches.

Neil Lomax
Phoenix Cardinals

ACKNOWLEDGMENTS

Rod and I would like to shine a light on those who made this book a reality.

Our deepest thanks to the following people:

Vic and Carolyn Bartruff, who introduced Bill to a word processor and helped make copies for the editors at Multnomah Press.

Gail Barram and Eva Gibson, who helped streamline and polish the manuscript.

The editors at Multnomah Press who brought this book from an idea to reality . . . Jane Aldrich Brown for seeing the need for this book, and Deena Davis for her persistence, expertise, and gentleness.

Eleanor Hunt, whose encouragement gave perseverance to an author before he became one.

Ken Voges, who shared his understanding of the Performax Personality Profile with Rod.

To the many individuals and small groups who were willing to offer their experiences and suggestions, especially to: The Lake Oswego Soccer Club, Kyle Rote Jr., Brad Bafaro, the Warddrip family, Bob and Judy Woodle, Jan and Ron Boyanovsky, Dave and Judi Carr.

INTRODUCTION

Several years ago a friend, Rod Cooper, helped me understand the uniqueness of children by highlighting for me their personality differences.

Nothing Rod said helped me more than his explanation of the Performax Profile System (PPS). Rod explained that all people fall into one of four basic personality styles. The PPS provides an easy way to identify and understand personality styles in others and in yourself.

The PPS divides people into two main categories and then further subdivides those into two groups. The two main categories are:

1) ACTIVE-EXTROVERT
2) LESS ACTIVE-INTROVERT

"Active-extroverts" make things happen. They don't adapt to their environment as much as they try to change it. They have definite ideas about how things should be and tend to direct people and circumstances to achieve them.

"Less active-introverts" prefer to adapt to their environment rather than change it. They focus more on the "why" and "how" of things and usually feel comfortable with the "status quo."

The "active-extrovert" category is subdivided into the:

PRODUCER parent/GO-GETTER child*
and
CHEERLEADER parent/PERSUADER child

The Producer parent and the Go-Getter child are both strongly dominant and goal-oriented. The Cheerleader parent and Persuader child tend to be more verbal, expressive, and relational.

The "less active-introvert" category is subdivided into the:

EXPERT parent/SPECIALIST child
and
IDEALIST parent/THINKER child

The Expert parent and the Specialist child seek peaceful relationships and are steady and predictable. The Idealist parent and Thinker child are both highly analytical and detail-oriented.

The stories in this book are based on the experience of my own children and of those on the teams I coached. Every story is true to the personality styles being described, but certain details have sometimes been altered to protect the privacy of those involved. If you think you recognize someone in the book, you don't—unless, of course, you see yourself or your children in the actions of others.

* For the purpose of this book, the personality titles of the PPS have been changed. A more complete explanation of the PPS is available in the appendix.

You may wonder how this work was co-authored. As I wrote of my experiences with parents, coaches, and children, Rod made sure the comments regarding behavioral styles were true to the Performax Profile System, and he provided the descriptive personality charts at the beginning of each chapter as well as the appendixes.

1

The Great Sports Migration

"Good Grief!" I blurted out to my wife, "Where did all these people come from?" Stretching before me was a school parking lot jammed with cars, a hundred kids or more kicking soccer balls across three fields, and a couple hundred watchful, eager parents.

Why had I never before seen this great social gathering? Actually, I had. But I never bothered to ask what it meant. Many times I had spotted bleachers filled with screaming parents at Little League baseball games. Often I had seen kids chasing a soccer ball while their parents cheered from the sidelines. But since my kids didn't play, I never thought much about it.

That all changed when my son came of age. It was then that I, like thousands of other parents, got pulled into The Great Sports Migration.

In late summer and continuing until early winter, soccer season takes over. Every Saturday from nine in the morning until three in the afternoon, hordes of vehicles bearing enthusiastic moms, dads, and athletes migrate to the athletic fields.

That's what brought me out to a crowded sideline years ago. My son, Ryan, was to play his first game. But something went wrong right away; the coach must have made some kind of mistake. *Coach, why isn't my son starting? Don't you know what a boring game this will be with him on the bench? And why are all these other parents so excited?*

I began to understand when my own freckle-faced six-year-old trotted onto the field. Suddenly I was transfixed. The action on the field was exciting, absorbing.

Throughout that first year I stood on the sidelines as a spectator. I knew nothing about soccer, but I knew I would learn. Within a year I found myself on the playing field itself, coaching a team of energetic kids.

Volunteering to coach gave me one of the greatest experiences of my life. It spotlighted many of my own strengths and weaknesses, and it has given me the chance to observe the strengths and weaknesses of many parents.

I had only been coaching a short while when I learned that what helped one kid often hurt another. I quickly saw that understanding both my own personality and the different personalities of children was critical for effective parenting and coaching.

My insight wasn't original. Thousands of years ago God urged the Jewish nation to train its children according to each child's uniqueness. That's what Solomon meant when he wrote in Proverbs 22:6:

Train a child in the way he should go, and when he is old he will not turn from it.

It surprises many to discover that Solomon wasn't exhorting parents to direct their children down a narrow path. Nor was he promising that, once old, children would return to that path. Rather, he wanted parents to train their children according to the individuality of each child.

A more literal translation of Proverbs 22:6 reads: "Train up a child in keeping with his way." The word for "way" is used elsewhere by Solomon to refer to the "way" of an eagle in flight, a snake on a rock, a ship on the sea, and a man with a woman (Proverbs 30:18, 19). Each of those four wonders enjoys a special beauty, something almost mysterious. Their "way" isn't a well-defined path but a unique characteristic which sets them apart.[1]

Solomon urged us to value the unique traits and characteristics of our children. He wanted our training to harmonize with the special traits of each child. Why? So that the child would accept the training and then, as he matured, be shaped by it.

The birth of a second child prompts every parent to notice one profound truth. How many times have you heard it said, "I can't believe how different those two are from one another"?

Unfortunately, while most parents know that each child is different from every other, they don't know precisely how to identify those differences. Consequently they tend to treat each child alike. "If I sit down and calmly reason with this child," they say, "then I should be able to calmly reason with the others." Or if they scream and yell at one, they scream and yell at the rest. Or if they reward one with praise, they reward the rest with praise. And so on.

The result? Some kids respond favorably and others don't. They actively or passively rebel.

Wouldn't parenting and coaching be a lot easier if every child responded identically? But they don't! Each child responds according to his or her unique wiring. Any wise parent or coach who strives for excellence will ask: "How can I better understand my children so that I can more effectively train them?"

Such understanding is critical when children and sports come together. Few settings emphasize the character flaws of a child more quickly than does athletic competition. A timid child will be reluctant to participate. An overly aggressive child will tend to dominate a game by refusing to pass the ball to a teammate.

Often parents stand on the sidelines and scream at their kids: "Kick the ball!" "Give the ball to someone else!" "Shoot!" "Play defense!" The poor kids aren't sure *what* to do.

It helps for a parent to know why a child acts in a certain way and what kind of support or correction works best with each child.

But there's another side to this coin. While it's easy to spot the weaknesses of a child who plays a sport, it's equally easy to identify the weaknesses of their parents. Most of us become suddenly transparent at a sporting event, especially if our child is playing. If you've ever been to a Little League baseball game, you know what I mean. Haven't most of us lost our cool because of a bad call by an umpire? Haven't we been guilty of itching to slam dunk the coach?

The truth is, we parents could use a little insight into ourselves as well as into our children.

But where do we begin? How can we better understand ourselves and our children so that we become better parents and supporters of our children?

Clearly, the place to begin is with ourselves. I'm convinced that after you've read the next four chapters, you'll not only know yourself better, but you'll have some specific ideas for improving as a parent and coach. The remainder of the book will help you to know your child better, much better. You'll also have a feel for how athletic competition, like a sculptor's tool, can be used to shape both you and your child into the image of Christ.

UNDERSTANDING
YOURSELF

THE PRODUCER

Strengths	Weaknesses
Produces immediate results	Insensitive to others
Makes quick decisions	Impatient
Persistent	Disregards risks
Problem-solver	Inflexible
Takes charge	Unyielding
Self-reliant	Takes on too much
Accepts challenges	Inattentive to detail
Goal-oriented	Demanding of others

Ideal environment:	Needs others to encourage:
New and varied activities	Sensitivity
Continual challenges	Caution
Difficult assignments	Attention to facts and details
Autonomy	
Control	
Direct answers	

2

The Producer

My first team just *had* to win. Immediately! Oh, I realized they were just second graders, but so what? I'd rather they win than lose.

To that end I recruited several high school soccer players and an experienced parent-coach as assistants. No doubt we had the best-coached second-grade team in Oregon. Destined for greatness!

Before our first game I worked up a chart showing when and where all of the kids would play; league rules required that each child play equal time.

When several players didn't show up on schedule, my carefully constructed plans evaporated. My chart was no longer any good; too many kids were missing. So I started the best players.

The missing players finally appeared, but in the excitement of the game I hardly noticed. They had missed a good chunk of the game by the time I realized they were available.

It didn't seem like a big deal to me. We won, didn't we? I had dreams of coaching a world cup team. And everybody was thrilled.

Well, not everybody. The father of one latecomer was fuming.

"Bill, I want you to know right now that I expect my daughter to play as much as anyone else!" Lon seethed. "I don't care if the team wins or loses, as long as she gets to play her two quarters!"

He didn't congratulate me for the victory. He didn't thank me for the great job I had done coaching the team. And I especially didn't like the tone of his voice.

I pulled out my chart and showed him how carefully I had planned on playing his daughter. I explained that when she showed up late it upset everything.

He replied (in words not appropriate for this book) that he didn't care about my chart, only about his daughter. And he expected her to play.

I'd never seen Lon so mad.

Later, a more experienced coach who had witnessed the scolding took me aside and offered his condolences. "Welcome to the league," he said, smiling. He pulled out a copy of another chart, better than mine, and handed it to me. With his chart a coach could figure out with just a glance how much a child had played.

When I got home I called Lon, apologized for not playing his daughter more, and told him about my new chart. He still wasn't thrilled about my chart, but he thanked me for calling.

The Motives of a Producer

The chart episode occurred after my first game. Since then I have coached or helped coach soccer, baseball, and basketball teams. I have discovered that my primary motive for coaching is a love for children. But deep within me rests another motivation. I love to win. I'm a Producer. That's true at work, home, and play. I remember a friend, a nationally-ranked wrestler, once saying, "Show me someone who likes to lose and I'll show you a loser." Well . . . I don't like to lose!

That competitive spirit followed me into children's sports. I found myself practicing soccer with my oldest son every day. I'm embarrassed to admit how immature I was. Imagine a thiry-two-year-old man forcing his second grade son to race through a dribbling obstacle course. Ryan hated it. Once he begged me to go home, but I refused. Instead I explained the importance of practice. Of course, I justified my actions: *Hey, he needs to get better. He needs to be a starter. I wouldn't admit that I had projected my ego needs onto him.*

I took that same attitude to my teams. Winning was more than important. It was necessary.

Unfortunately, that kind of unhealthy attitude afflicts others, too. You see the same competitive spirit wherever Little League is played. Producer parents often ruthlessly push their children to succeed. Some coaches talk to nine- and ten-year-old kids as though they played for World Series teams.

Understanding a Producer

What is it that drives Producer parents to win? Why are they so competitive? Why do they push their kids so hard?

It may surprise you to learn that in spite of confident appearances, many Producers fear exposure and rejection. At their innermost being many Producers fear they won't be accepted if they lose. And because Producers like to control their situations, they also fear they'll lose followers unless they consistently win.

That's why losing is so hard on Producers. They measure their significance by their win-loss record and compare their success to that of others. Whether it's at work, home, or play, it's hard for them to believe they could lose and still be okay. A Producer parent doesn't want to be seen as a loser. And they *sure* don't want their kids to be losers.

I've often searched my past for clues to help me understand my drive to win. I always felt close to both of my parents. I have fond memories of my dad coaching me in several sports. Indeed, some of my favorite childhood memories revolve around my dad teaching me to play baseball. Since I was the only boy in a family with four daughters, he poured himself into my life. And I loved him.

Yet, one thing I knew for sure: Dad expected me to win. I remember sometimes feeling that he'd be deeply disappointed if I didn't prove to be the best infielder or quarterback around. I wanted his approval, and I strove to win everything I could. But early on I realized something my father never did: I couldn't always win. There were guys bigger, faster, stronger, and more coordinated than me. Dad told me it didn't matter. He said practice could close the gap. I wasn't convinced, but I tried. I practiced and studied and worked and applied myself.

I tried to win, and sometimes I did. I competed in areas where I could win, and when I lost, I'd vow to try harder and practice longer and play smarter the next time around so that I would win. I wanted to win for Dad!

Don't get me wrong. I'm not implying that all Producer parents have had a childhood like mine. Still, if they look closely at their past, they'll probably find some reasons for their drive to win. In many instances that retrospective look will reveal a parent, relative, or coach whose approval flowed most freely when wins piled up the highest.

Producer Behavior

Nobody likes emotional pain, Producers included. Much of their behavior is aimed at preventing the pain associated with losing. Driven to win, Producers often become inconsiderate of anyone who gets in the way. That same drive also causes them to set ambitious goals.[2]

This passion to win causes Producers to persevere in the face of a challenge. Producers are determined, productive, and optimistic. Few things give them more pleasure than helping their own children or a team become champions.

Understanding the fears and actions of Producers won't necessarily strengthen their character or improve their behavior. But understanding does point out the basic fears they need to overcome. If you're a Producer, you must learn that your worth doesn't rest upon winning or losing. Realize there's a more important goal than winning.

An Effective Producer

Perhaps no one in the Bible better illustrates the strengths and weaknesses of a Producer than the apostle Paul. It's also Paul who best illustrates the transformation of an intense competitor into a man of compassion.

Before his conversion, Paul was called Saul. Driven to win, Saul of Tarsus spent much of his life trying to prove to the religious community that he was a great and godly leader. When it came to orthodoxy, Saul meant his viewpoint to prevail. How did he keep score? By counting the numbers of Christians he could find and destroy. As a Jewish zealot he sought to persecute those he believed to be spreading a false religion (Acts 9:1, 2).

Then one day on a road leading to Damascus, Saul met the risen Christ. A transformation took place. His life suddenly took on new meaning and his fears dissolved. So radical was the change that God gave him a new name, Paul. Repeatedly thereafter this transformed man wrote about the force which both drove and directed his life.

No longer was Paul driven by a fear of failure. "Therefore, there is now no condemnation for those who are in Christ Jesus" he told the Romans (Romans 8:1). Paul learned there was nothing he could do to win God's favor, and he discovered no failure of his would cause God to reject him.

When confidence replaced fear, Paul discovered a vital purpose for living. As a Producer he still had lofty goals which he strove to achieve. But the nature of his goals changed. He expressed it to some friends like this: ". . . whatever you do, do it all to the glory of God . . . even as I try to please everybody in every way. For I am not seeking my own good but the good of many, so that they may be saved" (1 Corinthians 10:31, 33).

Before he became a Christian, sympathy was not one of Saul's strong points. He viewed people as allies or enemies, and he strategically used his allies to destroy his enemies (Acts 9:1, 2). His contacts with high-ranking religious officials meant he had no trouble obtaining the official documents needed to accomplish his goal—the arrest of Christians. Saul didn't care whose families he disrupted or whose lives he destroyed.

But then he was converted, and everywhere he went he urged believers to demonstrate love and compassion. The apostle wrote of his love for the

Thessalonians when he said in 1 Thessalonians 2:7, 8:

> *But we were gentle among you, like a mother caring for*
> *her little children. We loved you so much that we were*
> *delighted to share with you not only the gospel of God but*
> *our lives as well, because you had become so dear to us.*

Do his words sound like those of a Producer? Hardly. Oh, Paul still had a lofty goal: To impart the gospel, to glorify God. But by this point a deep compassion for the people of Thessalonica throbbed in his heart.

The apostle soon learned the importance of affirmation as he scurried about the world building churches. Perhaps no New Testament epistle illustrates this commitment more than First Corinthians. Immorality, pride, and divisiveness filled the church at Corinth. Believers got drunk during communion; one man had gone to bed with his stepmother. Yet, when Paul wrote these people, he began with words of affirmation (1 Corinthians 1:1-9).

Proper Goals

Prompted by a passion to glorify God by bringing others to Christ, Paul subordinated everything to that single purpose. Producer parents and coaches constantly need to remind themselves why they're coaching and why their kids are playing.

At the beginning of my coaching career, several friends were concerned that my desire to win might drive me to push the kids too hard. Realizing the danger was real, I determined early on that my coaching would serve as an opportunity for personal growth. Not only did I want to help my sons develop character, but I wanted to grow myself. To enhance my own development as a father and coach I set a threefold goal:

1) To replace my fear of losing with a confident trust in God;

2) To honor God with my actions and words;

3) To help my children have fun while developing their athletic skills and character.

Those three goals became the driving force behind my coaching. Soon they also became crucial to my role as father. There's not much difference between coaching a team and leading a family, for both require the same kind of sensitivity and balance.

Still, having honorable goals in no way ensures their accomplishment. It might help to write on a three-by-five card:

MY GOAL IS TO
TRUST GOD WITH MY FEARS
HONOR HIM
HELP MY CHILDREN

Every time you find yourself pushing your children or players too hard, pull out that card and read it. You'll be surprised how it helps keep your mind on the right track. Overcoming an obsessive drive to win demands discipline. It requires dealing with your fears and focusing on a higher goal, a more important game. But it also requires a change in how you view people.

Cultivate Compassion

A Producer's premium on winning often inflicts great pain on his or her children and players. Several years ago I coached a boy who did a great job playing goalie, even though he didn't enjoy the position. About halfway through the season, Skip, his dad, urged me to take Josh out of the goalie box.

I listened, but I knew Josh had to play goalie if we were to win. I thought I had appeased Josh when I promised to let him play another position if we got a big lead.

The next season I discovered how much that decision had discouraged Josh. He chose to play on a Junior League Football team rather than play soccer.

Skip later assured me that Josh loved football and had always wanted to play.

"That may be," I said. "But I regret leaving him at goalie when he wanted to play elsewhere. After all, he was just a fourth grader."

At a higher level players often become locked into a position, but by that time they've usually developed expertise in it and prefer it. Fourth graders, on the other hand, need the freedom to find a position they enjoy.

Why didn't I honor Josh's request to play elsewhere? The answer's simple. As a Producer, my desire to win washed away my compassion.

I must constantly remind myself that a child's feelings are more important than winning. However, being aware of another's feelings isn't the same as showing compassion, because compassion isn't a technique to be mastered but a sensitivity to be demonstrated. It requires an awareness that both a player and his parents are needy and fearful. A child doesn't want to fail, yet he fears failure and the rejection which accompanies it.

Josh didn't want to play goalie because goalies don't kick goals. They try to stop them. And one careless mistake in the goalie box could cost a victory.

What about Josh's parents? They wanted their son in the middle of the action. They wanted him in a position which would build his self-esteem . . . and theirs.

A Producer coach must ask God for the wisdom to view players as individuals with fears and needs, not as pawns in a chess game. Active listening which avoids quick solutions and easy answers lets kids know they're accepted. With that feeling of acceptance they become free to improve their skills, take chances, and make mistakes without fear of rejection. A child needs to know there is hope despite personal limitations.

Few Producer coaches view themselves as nursing mothers who give their players emotional nourishment as well as athletic training. Yet compassion and love must be expressed if a Producer is to strengthen personal parenting and coaching skills.

Only through prayer and conscious effort can such a change occur. It demands a daily choice to remember that players are people. It requires a conscious recall of the fears and needs of those being coached or parented. It means taking the time to listen.

Such decisions are easier to make than keep. There will be times when compassion seems to get in the way of winning. Then, faith becomes the issue.

Producers tend to trust in personal drive to achieve success. That's what motivated Paul prior to his conversion. But God urges us to trust in him; he wants us to do what's right and to rely upon him for the outcome.

In God's eyes, compassion is more important than winning. Not a mushy kind of compassion that avoids tough decisions, but the kind that enables Producer coaches to understand the children they coach.

What About Criticism?

Nobody likes criticism. It stings. The tongue-lashing I received after my first soccer game hurt. I felt like handing my clipboard to Lon and saying: "Here, you coach the team!"

Yet because I'm a Producer, Lon's straightforward approach was best for me.

Unfortunately, Producers—since they don't need an ego massage before being corrected—tend to treat others with the same curtness appropriate to their own dispositions. When they see a problem with a player they just tell them how to correct it.[3] Too often they forget sensitivity and affirmation.

Producer parents and coaches must concentrate on affirming their children and players. I consciously try to give a word of praise before and after each criticism. Remember the "sandwich" method of correcting a player: Place the criticism between two slices of praise.

Above my desk at home hangs a small wooden and bronze plaque bearing the inscription:

MANY THANKS
COACH PERKINS
L.O.S.C. LEAGUE CHAMPS

Beneath those words, handwritten in bronze, are the signatures of each player. As I read those names I mentally see each child's face, recall each personality, savoring each one as though gazing at pictures in a great gallery.

The pleasure of games won has long since faded. But the memory of skills taught, character developed, and friendships started remains.

I hope the process of growth continues for each of them. I hope it continues for me. Sure, winning is fun . . . but cultivating character in children is better, more lasting, and a far superior goal.

ON THE PRACTICE FIELD

1. If you're a Producer, try to listen to the complete story before making a decision (Proverbs 18:12, 13).

2. Understand that every situation isn't competitive (Proverbs 18:1, 20.

3. Resist fighting back when corrected. Look at correction as a way to grow and mature (Hebrews 12:5-11).

BASIC FEAR: *Being viewed as a loser.*

KEY VERSE: *"I delight in weaknesses, in insults, in hardships, in persecutions, in difficulties. For when I am weak, then I am strong"*
(2 Corinthians 12:10).

THE CHEERLEADER

Strengths

Optimistic
Enthusiastic
Personable
Makes a favorable impression
Articulate
Desires to help others
Entertaining

Weaknesses

Lacks follow-through
Oversells
Overestimates results
Misjudges capabilities
Acts impulsively
Jumps to conclusions
Overcommits

Ideal environment:

Friendly atmosphere
Freedom from detail
Opportunity to influence
Public recognition
Opportunity to talk
Excitement about ideas

Needs other to encourage:

Follow-through
A logical approach
Concentration on a task

3

The Cheerleader

Impressive was the word for Jay's meticulously manicured lawn. It looked as though someone had taken a pair of scissors and neatly clipped every blade of grass, applying hair spray to each one. The assorted hedges along the front of the house blended so well I wondered if Jay had chosen the colors from a designer catalog. Everything, absolutely everything about his house flashed one word: STYLE. Even his shiny red Porsche complemented the scene like a silk scarf tucked into the breast pocket of a classy double-breasted suit.

As my 1978 Olds Cutlass entered his circular driveway, Jay bounded out the front door. Before I could shut off the engine and climb out, he ran over to my car, opened my door, and announced breathlessly, "I've got a video of the game. How'd you like to watch it?"

Oh no! I thought, *this could be a long afternoon.*

"Actually, Jay, I'm kinda pressed for time and would rather have you tell me about the game," I said.

"Come on, Bill!" he protested. "You'd enjoy watching them on TV." He grabbed my arm and directed me toward his house.

"Who won?" I asked.

"Hey, I don't want to take away the suspense," he said. You'll see for yourself."

Sandy, Jay's wife, saw us coming. "Are you showing Bill that video? Because if you are, you'd better tell him your coaching cost us the championship."

"You mean you lost?" I asked.

"We sure did," Sandy replied. "And you should have seen how mad the parents were at Jay. Everyone blamed him."

"Actually," Jay said, "we lost the game because of John, my assistant. I gave him responsibility for the lineup. Even though his boy had never played point guard, he left him in at that position the entire game."

"Right," Sandy said, "and why didn't you change the lineup?"

"Because I didn't want to offend John. He'd done a good job all season," Jay answered.

He slipped the cartridge into the VCR unit.

"Here's the pre-game pep talk. I always did a super job preparing the kids."

"Jay," I asked, "who did the video?"

"Oh, we hired a professional," Jay answered. "He's also the fella doing the play-by-play analysis of the game."

"You hired a professional photographer to film a first grade basketball game? Come on, Jay, tell me you're kidding!"

"Bill, this was a championship game. The parents wanted a record of it."

"Wait a minute," Sandy interjected. "You're the one who insisted on hiring a professional and then sold the idea to the parents."

"What do you mean? Everybody thought it was a great idea! I just did what they wanted. Besides, we got a good video. Hey Bill, listen to this pep talk."

The camera zeroed in on Jay: "Okay boys, if you do your best you're a winner regardless of the final score. So get out there! Hustle! Play your best!"

Instantly I realized I was watching a classic Cheerleader coach at work. Jay was wonderful with words. He regularly affirmed his players, even those who played poorly. And hadn't he talked the parents into hiring a professional to film the game?

Unfortunately, Jay also demonstrated a Cheerleader's weaknesses. After showing up late for the game and failing to plan the lineup, he later avoided making changes that might have helped the team. Why? Because he didn't want to offend his assistant coach.

Cheerleading at Mt. Sinai

The best Old Testament illustration of a Cheerleader may be Aaron. He and his brother Moses were called by God to deliver the Israelites from slavery in Egypt. Their story, found in the book of Exodus, shows the strengths and weaknesses of a Cheerleader.

Each man's unique gifts came out by working with the other. Moses had a mind aimed at precision and detail. Aaron possessed unusual communication skills. What Moses lacked, Aaron possessed, and vice versa. Buoyed by the faith of Moses and by the support of God, Aaron risked everything when he stood before Pharoah and insisted that the people of God be released. In that moment, his skills as an effective communicator were put to their highest use.

Days later, when Moses climbed Mt. Sinai to receive the Law, Aaron the Cheerleader was left in charge of the people. Forty days and forty nights passed without anyone hearing anything from Moses, and finally, restless and impatient, the people approached Aaron and said, "Make us gods who will go before us. As for this fellow Moses who brought us up out of Egypt, we don't know what has happened to him" (Exodus 32:1).

Without any recorded effort to resist, Aaron built an idol and said, "These are your gods, O Israel, who brought you up out of Egypt." The following day he led the people in worshiping that golden calf (Exodus 32:1-6).

When Moses came down from the mountain and saw the people worshiping an idol, he asked Aaron, "What did these people do to you, that you led them into such great sin?"

Aaron replied, "They said to me, 'Make us gods who will go before us. As for this fellow Moses who brought us up out of Egypt, we don't know what has happened to him.' So I told them, 'Whoever has any gold jewelry, take it off.' Then they gave me the gold, and I threw it into the fire, and out came this calf!" (Exodus 32:23-24).

Notice that Aaron held the people and the fire responsible for the golden calf. Perhaps he thought that by blaming the fire he could avoid further angering either Moses or the people. Cheerleader personalities often use their ability with words to shift responsibility onto others.

Understanding a Cheerleader

Why are Cheerleaders so like floating balloons, blown about by shifting winds of popular opinion? Why do they find it so hard to accept responsibility for their actions? Why do they tend to lack punctuality and organization? The answer lies in understanding their inner motivations.

People Oriented

Jay's lack of organization, punctuality, and follow-through sometimes are caused by congeniality. Occasionally he gets so wrapped up in talking with friends that he loses track of time and forgets what he's doing.

"It's hard for me to pull away from a conversation," Jay says. "Once I begin talking with someone, I'm afraid they'll be hurt if I tell them I have to go."

Fearful

Surprisingly, Jay's friendliness masks a fear of exposure and rejection. Jay, like other Cheerleaders, wants to be viewed as entertaining, friendly, and successful. Yet at his core he struggles with feelings of weakness and inferiority. He fears others will see his weakness and reject him.

His need to avoid the pain of rejection motivates Jay to display the trappings of success. While there's nothing inherently wrong with owning nice things, Jay frequently buys toys on credit because he hasn't the money to pay for them.

Jay's appetite for the symbols of success may cause him to push his kids to do well athletically, scholastically, and socially. Jay knows the achievements of his children reflect positively on him.

Easily Directed

Cheerleaders tend to allow others to direct their actions. Why? Because their deep inner pain is quickly soothed by the laughter and praise of friends. Unfortunately, when the laughter dies and the compliments fade, the pain returns. In an effort to soothe the ache, Cheerleaders listen to multiplying demands and seek to meet them. They want to please everyone. Eventually they say "yes" to anyone, including themselves and their children.[4]

An Effective Cheerleader

When I kidded Jay about blaming John for the lost game, he laughed, then turned serious. "The hardest thing for me about getting married was seeing myself through Sandy's eyes," he said. "I'd been pretty good at finding excuses for most of my problems. But she wouldn't buy them. Once, while in college, I charged some clothes and told her I needed them for work. Sandy saw right through me and said, 'Jay, your boss hasn't said anything about your clothes. You're just wrapped up in always looking good, and you're impulsive. You saw those clothes, wanted them, and spent money we don't have.'"

Understand Your Fears

While Jay admitted Sandy's words hurt, he also acknowledged that they forced him into deep introspection, something he seldom did. He realized he had grown up in a family where parents put a premium on expensive cars and nice clothes.

"They convinced me that if I looked sharp and drove a nice car I'd be successful. Consequently, I grew up judging people by outward appearances."

Jay's earliest memories of impulsive behavior weren't about lavish purchases, however. "Early on I learned that I could make people laugh," he said. "It felt good. In elementary school I was the class clown."

Jay refused to restrain his humor in the classroom; he spoke out, interrupting the teacher and disrupting the class.

"I didn't know it," Jay said, "but I think the laughter kept me from looking inward and dealing with my feelings of inadequacy."

Jay was lucky—Sandy forced him to look inward. She didn't laugh off his impulsive behavior. She didn't accept his false excuses. She loved him unconditionally while helping him face his failures and fears.

Such introspection hurts a Cheerleader. It's difficult to admit feelings of inadequacy. It's painful to admit that fear sometimes motivates a friendliness aimed more at self-protection than at helping others. Yet such introspection is crucial if a Cheerleader is to grow.

Assume Responsibility

Most Cheerleaders would rather avoid introspection and the pain of criticism than accept correction. They tend to blame others. That's why they must learn to accept responsibility for their own actions.

That's exactly what Moses forced Aaron to do. He dealt with his Cheerleader brother and the rest of the nation by holding everyone responsible for their actions. Effective correction of Cheerleaders focuses on what they have said or done, regardless of what others did to contribute to the problem.

"She wouldn't let me off the hook," Jay says of Sandy's loving confrontation. "I squirmed and dodged, but eventually I had to face the truth about myself. Oh, I still struggle with wanting nice things. I want to impress people. But I've dealt better with my problem since I've begun to understand it. I constantly remind myself that God accepts me just as I am. I know that sounds trite, but consciously looking to the Lord for acceptance requires mental discipline."

Occasionally that discipline slips away from Jay. He remembers recruiting an assistant coach, coming up with a team plan, and then allowing three more dads to help coach the team. The kids didn't know who to listen to. Why had Jay done it? "I didn't want any of the dads to feel left out," he said.

Fortunately for Jay, Sandy gives him strength. She helps him think before acting and then reminds him to follow through. When she sees him wrapped up in pleasing his friends she confronts him. Sometimes he even listens.

Follow-Through

Cheerleader coaches are best balanced by assistants or spouses who are Idealists or Experts. Why? Because Idealists and Experts make sure details get carried out. They help with the follow-through. Still, recruiting a good assistant only provides a temporary solution. Cheerleader parents and coaches must develop their own eye for detail. They need to guard themselves against mental lapses.

Instead of "winging it" at practice, they should plan out practices ahead of time. If you're a Cheerleader, ask yourself, "What do my players need to learn this season?" Devise a practice schedule which will allow you to systematically teach your players what they need to learn.

At home, don't just tell your kids how they can improve in school or sports, sit down with them and lay out a strategy. Then check with them on a daily basis. Ask how they're doing with their reading, spelling, tennis, or soccer practice. Better yet, read with them or practice a sport with them.

Ask God for the grace needed to maintain friendliness while following through with the details, even unpleasant details. Meet regularly with your assistant coach to discuss team practices. If he is detail oriented, he'd be glad to work with you and he'll blossom under your attention. After all, you are the motivator . . . the heart of the team.

Accent the Positive

A Cheerleader's ability to see the potential in children is the power to shape young lives. It's an awesome responsibility and a great privilege.

Remember the story of Paul and Barnabas? The pre-Christian Saul hunted down Christians and threw them into jail (Acts 9:1, 2). He approved of the stoning of Stephen and even held the robes of those who threw the rocks (Acts 7:58). The disciples therefore had good reason to question this man's sincerity when he first professed to be a Christian. What if Paul was only pretending to be a Christian so he could trap more believers?

But one man listened. One man saw Paul's need to be accepted by the church. One man had been known for consistently offering praise and hope to his friends. That man was called Joseph the Levite, but the apostles changed his name to Barnabas, which in Greek means "Son of Encouragement."

Barnabas, the Son of Encouragement, stood beside Paul and told the early church leaders about his friend's conversion. Barnabas explained that Paul had spoken out boldly in the name of Jesus. As a result, the disciples accepted him (Acts 9:27-31).

Barnabas and Paul continued to work together for many years, despite suffering their share of disagreements. None proved more bitter than that concerning John Mark. Paul refused to take the boy with him on his second missionary journey because John Mark had deserted him while ministering in Pamphylia. Moved by compassion, Barnabas refused to leave John Mark behind. So the two of them traveled to Cyprus while Paul left with Silas for Syria and Cilicia. Cheerleader Barnabas was committed to seeing other people succeed, and he was willing to take risks with Paul and later with Mark because he believed in them.

Years later, while in prison, Paul wrote to Timothy, "Get Mark and bring him with you, because he is helpful to me in my ministry" (2 Timothy 4:11b). Apparently a transformation had taken place. Mark had grown through the encouragement he received from Barnabas. And Paul, who once had been championed by Barnabas, saw the hand of his old friend at work in Mark's life and therefore saw the young man's worth.

If you're a Cheerleader coach or parent, you have been wonderfully gifted to bring out the best in people. Find a John Mark who needs someone to believe in him. Encourage that child and watch God use your words of praise to shape him or her into a winner.

ON THE PRACTICE FIELD

1. If you are a Cheerleader, be aware of conforming to social pressure (1 Corinthians 10:13).

2. Be conscious of talking too much (Proverbs 10:19).

3. Be sure to finish what you start (Proverbs 10:5).

4. Beware of shifting the blame to others or to circumstances when things go wrong (Proverbs 21:2).

BASIC FEAR: *Being viewed as unsuccessful.*

KEY VERSE: *"The LORD does not look at the things man looks at. Man looks at the outward appearance, but the LORD looks at the heart"*
(1 Samuel 16:7b).

THE EXPERT

Strengths

Supportive
Agreeable
Loyal
Self-controlled
Consistent
Good listener
Performs set work patterns well

Weaknesses

Resists change
Difficulty with deadlines
Overly tolerant
Indecisive
Holds grudges
Possessive
Lacks initiative

Ideal Environment:

Appreciation
Freedom from conflict
Security
Affirmation for a job well done
Limited responsibility
Stable relationships

Needs others to encourage:

Risk-taking
Facing difficult problems
Self-motivation

4

The Expert

Carol has a tough time disciplining kids. Once when she saw her youngest son, Todd, throwing rocks against the house, she walked into the back yard and asked him to stop. A few minutes later she glanced out the kitchen window and couldn't believe her eyes. Todd was about to throw another rock against the house. She raced across the kitchen just as her husband, Jeff, walked through the front door.

"What's going on?" he asked.

Carol yelled a brief explanation and then headed for Todd.

"But Mom," he said, "You told me not to throw rocks! I'm not—I'm throwing pebbles!"

He opened his little hand and showed Carol the pebbles. She looked at those pleading brown eyes and melted.

She told Todd she didn't want him throwing rocks, pebbles, clods, boulders, or any other hard objects in the back yard. And she let him go.

"Later," Carol said, "Jeff told me I was a softie. He didn't buy Todd's explanation and urged me to discipline him. Somehow Jeff could see disobedience clearly and deal with it quickly. That's always been hard for me. I'm more of a peacemaker, and the kids often take advantage of my gullibility. Come to think of it, so do adults."

Carol's blue eyes sparkled as she remembered one particular example of people taking advantage of her: The evening she unexpectedly became a Little League baseball coach.

"I'd been told the parents planned to discuss the upcoming season. I arrived early with no more knowledge of what was to come than Custer had prior to the battle of Little Big Horn.

"Once there I ate a finger snack and chatted with the other parents. When Jim Boyanovsky called us all into the family room, I missed a strategic opportunity to escape. But at that point I didn't know I'd need to.

"Following a brief discussion about the previous year's record, Jim said, 'Folks, I'm afraid we don't have a coach. I've talked with all the dads and none of them are able to coach the team this season.'"

Carol began to feel she had been lured into a friendly trap. When Jim asked if she had played sports in college, she knew she'd been set up.

"Sure, I played tennis in college," she told Jim. "Why do you ask?"

Of course, she knew why she'd been asked.

"Well, Carol," Jim said with a smile, "We wondered if you'd be willing to coach the team."

"Wait a minute, Jim, I played *tennis* in college. Not baseball! There's no way I'd ever coach a sport I hadn't mastered."

"Now Carol, before you say 'No!' just listen to me. A number of the other parents have agreed to help if you'll be the head coach. Besides, you've played softball, haven't you?"

"Jim, I played on the church softball team. That doesn't qualify me to coach Little League, even if it's a minor league team!"

"Sure it does," Jim said. "Especially if you have several dads helping you. Come on, Carol, you're our only hope. The rest of us won't let you down. Honest!"

The gentle persuasion of her friends eventually overcame her reluctance, and Carol agreed to coach the team—but only after one of the dads agreed to help.

"Usually when I allow people to pressure me into doing something I live to regret it," Carol confessed. "As I drove home that night I hoped I wouldn't be sorry for agreeing to coach. I knew I didn't know what I was doing, so I attended some coaching clinics to learn the basics of fielding and hitting. Throwing batting practice proved impossible; I just couldn't pitch strikes. Whenever I tried I felt spastic. Fortunately, Jim helped out in that area."

Carol's high standards normally push her to avoid involvement in anything she hasn't mastered. But those same standards can motivate study, practice, and hard work in a new area to which she commits herself.

"I think I surprised the other parents," Carol said of that first coaching year. "They didn't expect such diligence on my part. The kids had a winning season because we practiced so frequently."

Carol, like other Experts, fears the rejection which can result from failure or discord. She agreed to coach in order to avoid dissension and to win her friends' acceptance. Experts tend to be overly tolerant and agreeable, and their gentle spirit is attractive to others. Unfortunately, an Expert's desire to avoid conflict sometimes prompts unwise decisions.

Abraham and Isaac: Two Experts

Frustrated that she remained childless, Sarai asked Abram to allow Hagar, her handmaid, to bear them a child. "And Abram agreed" it says in the Living Bible (Genesis 16:2b). So Abram slept with Hagar.

Neither Sarai or Abram stopped to count the cost of their decision. Sarai's pain of remaining childless soon seemed insignificant compared to the agony caused by Hagar's pregnancy. Once pregnant, Hagar became arrogant. The handmaid considered herself better than Sarai. From Hagar's viewpoint, God had blessed her with a child while Sarai remained barren.

Burning with anger, Sarai scolded Abram and said, "It's all your fault" (Genesis 16:5 Living Bible).

And how did Abram respond? Rather than dealing with his own sin and that of his wife, he took the course of least resistance. He gave Sarai permission to punish Hagar. Sarai beat Hagar soundly (Genesis 16:6). Emotionally broken, Hagar ran away into the wilderness.

Years later, Abraham's son, Isaac, would follow in some of his father's footsteps. He, too, would discover the dangers of being too agreeable.

A famine had stripped the land of vegetation. Storehouses of grain ran empty, and Isaac's livestock, servants, and children faced a painful, prolonged death.

What should he do? Then he remembered: Didn't his father once survive a famine by traveling south to Gerar? Well, so would he.

Isaac's agreeable personality enabled him to develop friendly relations with most everyone he met. He even prospered among an otherwise hostile group, the Philistines (Genesis 26:1-6). But when social pressures arose, his gracious personality led him to take the path of least resistance.

Rebekah, Isaac's wife, possessed great beauty and charm. Isaac knew her looks might bring trouble with the Philistines, since kings in ancient times often killed for women they found attractive. So Isaac said she was his sister. To avoid strife, Isaac lied and thus jeopardized his wife's virtue. (Genesis 26:7-11).

Improving As an Expert

What motivates Experts to avoid conflict and seek peaceful relationships?

Experts have an intense fear of exposure and rejection. By now, you may have noticed that the basic fear for each personality type has been exposure and rejection. However, the way each personality type behaves as a result of the core fear is unique.

Experts view themselves as weak and inadequate, and in an effort to prevent others from seeing their inadequacy, they do everything possible to demonstrate their competency. They try so hard to please others that they often overcompensate. Experts hope an excellent performance will shield their weaknesses from view.

Understand Your Fears

How do Experts measure their success? They evaluate their performance by the response of others. Anything other than a peaceful relationship tells them they have failed. If those they want to impress respond negatively, Experts suffer extreme emotional pain. To erase that pain or to prevent it from recurring, they will either avoid the person who hurt them or vow to do better the next time.

Carol remembers a particularly painful incident in her childhood. Her second grade teacher asked Carol to make a class announcement.

All of the students were "acting up," and Carol was expected to get them quiet. No one listened.

For several minutes Carol tried to silence the unruly class. Finally the teacher walked to the front of the room, gave Carol a look of disgust, and said, "If you can't make the announcement, then I'll do it for you."

"I felt like a total failure," Carol said. "As the tears rolled down my cheeks I told myself I'd never let that happen again."

Carol's childhood experience was intensified by the hand-me-down clothes her parents gave her in an attempt to save money.

"I never felt I measured up to the other students," she said. "I made good grades, played some sports, and was friendly. I hoped the other kids would like me, but I always felt a little inferior."

Carol the Adult finds it hard to say no when her friends pressure her, yet when she does what they want, she fears they will see her inadequacy and reject her. She's often more concerned with being liked by her kids than doing what's right. That's why she finds it easy to overlook disobedience.

Expert parents and coaches need to recognize that avoiding strife may sacrifice opportunities to develop character, either in themselves or in their children.[5]

How did God address the fears of Abraham and Isaac? Time and again God renewed his promises to them. The Lord allowed both men to get dragged into situations where they would fail and then assured them of his love. When Abram allowed Sarai to mistreat Hagar, God intervened and protected Hagar (Genesis 16:7-13). And when Isaac lied about Rebekah, God stepped in to keep her from harm. Later, God prospered Isaac. We read: "Isaac planted crops in that land and the same year reaped a hundredfold, because the LORD blessed him" (Genesis 26:12).

God showed both Abraham and Isaac that his blessings were not directly related to either man's ability to perform well or win his pleasure.

In one instance God placed Abraham in a crisis where he had no choice but to fight. In that confrontation Abraham led his small army against a much larger force, but God gave him victory.

When at last Abraham learned to trust God with his fears, the Lord commanded the patriarch to sacrifice his son. If ever Abraham ran the risk of conflict, he faced it now! But Abraham had learned he could endure conflict if he was acting in obedience to God's will, and he knew that pleasing others (even himself) isn't the most important thing in life.

Like Abraham and Isaac, Expert parents and coaches must consciously remember to trust God in the face of change, during conflict, and when asked to perform in areas where they lack experience.[6] They must remember that their personal worth doesn't rest upon the approval of others.

Overcome Your Fears

Learning to deal with fear of rejection hasn't been easy for Carol. As a Little League coach she was forced to deal with "a problem child." It seemed every time Carol's son, Todd, and a friend, Bob, got together at practice, they fed each other's disrespect. After every effort failed to peacefully control the boy, Carol faced a terrifying reality: She would have to talk with Bob's parents.

Carol knew that Bob's mother and father liked to present themselves as perfect parents and Bob as an ideal child. She felt certain they would be defensive.

"Sure enough," Carol said, "they told me the problem wasn't with their son, but with Todd. I assured them I knew Todd had a problem, but also let them know Bob showed disrespect for authority and frequently disrupted our practices.

"I felt terrible after our meeting. I just knew they hated me. But I did what had to be done. Amazingly, Bob's behavior improved and his parents acted as though nothing had happened. My worst fears were never realized."

If you're an Expert parent you probably know how hard it is to discipline your children. It's easier for you to let problems roll off your back. You also may struggle with talking through difficulties with your spouse. Yet, like Carol, you must learn to do

what's right regardless of how others may feel
about your actions. You must learn that standing
up for what's right is often more important than
keeping everyone happy.

Experts also fear they won't perform perfectly.
Carol suffered from this when she agreed to coach.
She wanted to please the other parents but was
nervous because she had never coached baseball.
She fears a poor performance may disappoint
others and cause her own rejection. That's a risk
Experts avoid.

Expert parents and coaches, like Carol, must
consciously remember to trust God during times of
conflict, even minor conflicts. At home, disobedience must be addressed quickly. At team practices, disrespectful children must be challenged
and corrected. Tension may be the result, but
avoiding conflict doesn't make the problem go
away; it only intensifies future conflicts. Just ask
Abraham.

"I still hate conflict and avoid it when I can,"
Carol said. "But I know that with God's help I can
stand up for what's right and be okay. I have to
remind myself that God won't let me down when I
face new challenges or difficult people."

When faced with new and unexpected challenges, Experts should try to avoid concentrating
on their inability to perfectly fulfill new obliga-
tions. Instead, trust in the Lord to give you
strength and wisdom to do your best. Remember,

Paul told the Corinthians that God demands faithfulness of his servants, not perfection (1 Corinthians 4:2). Seek to gain God's pleasure more than that of your friends.

Carol eventually learned that she didn't have to be a professional to coach a Little League team.

"We didn't win the league championship, but we did pretty well," she said. "The kids enjoyed the season and so did the parents. I even managed to help the boys improve their game.

"I treasure my memory of the appreciation party the parents threw for our baseball team. After they had given the kids all of the little trophies, they gave me a sweatshirt with my name and the words SUPER COACH written in bold print.

"I realize I'm no super coach. But I also know if I'd never taken a chance and coached that team, I wouldn't have known the joy of loving and helping those kids. Now, when I face a threatening challenge, I pull that sweatshirt out of the closet and put it on. It's a reminder to me that God can be trusted, and I need all those reminders I can get."

ON THE PRACTICE FIELD

1. There are no "dumb" questions. If you don't know, that's okay (James 1:5).

2. Try not to internalize anger or use silence as a weapon (Ephesians 4:30-32).

3. Meditate upon Psalm 56:3, 4b: "When I am afraid, I will trust in you. In God I trust: I will not be afraid. What can mortal man do to me?"

The words of that psalm offer courage during moments of crisis. I'd suggest you make those verses a subject of daily meditation. As you meditate upon them, imagine those circumstances in which you tend to seek human support and affirmation. Think through how you would trust God for strength during such times.

BASIC FEAR: *Being viewed as weak.*

KEY VERSE: *"I can do everything through him who gives me strength"* (Philippians 4:13).

THE IDEALIST

Strengths

Orderly
Conscientious
Disciplined
Precise
Thorough
Diplomatic
Analytical

Weaknesses

Indecisive
Overattention to detail
Rigid
Avoids conflict
Hesitant to try new things
Avoids full responsibility
Pessimistic

Ideal Environment:

Detail-oriented
Stable surroundings
Reassurance and affirmation
Clear understanding of expectations
Time for planning
Commitment to quality

Needs others to encourage:

Decision-making behavior
Self-confidence
Optimistic point of view

5

The
Idealist

Don was so mad he almost jerked the phone off the wall. He had coached his son's team for three years, and now, without warning, they had asked him to resign.

I'd never seen Don so hurt or angry. He'd been told that a former pro player had volunteered to coach the team and the club officers couldn't pass up such an offer—but the reasoning didn't ring true. Don's team had won the regional championship the year before. His dismissal made him the first coach to win a championship one year and get the boot the next. Indeed, never before had the league dismissed a volunteer coach.

What had caused the forced resignation? Don later admitted that his leaving was good for the team: "I never felt qualified to coach the boys. I didn't volunteer for the job; they recruited me because my teams always won."

But were there other reasons the club had replaced Don? Almost certainly. Often when parents approached him with concerns about his coaching, Don refused to listen and instead demanded that the parents list specific grievances. The parents seldom went into detail but rather vaguely referred to attitude problems they had seen in their kids. Hurt, Don wrote himself a job description and distributed it. Then he kept a careful record of his adherence to what he'd written.

At practices Don concentrated on a few fundamentals and offered little variety. When his players complained of boredom he told them he would teach new drills when they perfected the old ones. Don's eye for detail didn't allow the slightest mistake to pass without notice or criticism. During games he struggled with occasional outbursts of anger at players who failed to perform perfectly.

Because Don had talented athletes on his team, the few skills they mastered enabled them to consistently win. But when the club officers wanted the children to learn new skills, Don refused to budge. He believed his methods succeeded, and he refused to teach any new techniques.

So when the former pro player stepped onto the scene, Don was shown the back door. In a conciliatory gesture the president of the club gave Don another team of younger players, and it wasn't long before those kids had mastered the skills needed to win.

At home it was little different. Don liked things done the right way—*his* way.

"Sure l knew there were two ways to squeeze a tube of toothpaste; but why waste toothpaste?" he asked. "I tried for months to convince my wife that squeezing the tube from the bottom wouldn't work as well as rolling it up" (No kidding! The toothpaste tube issue seemed clear to Don).

Eventually, Don's wife bought two tubes: one for Don to squeeze "the right way" and the other for her to squeeze from the bottom.

Moses the Idealist

Like Don, Moses didn't volunteer for the job. He never asked God to make him the deliverer of Israel. Moses actually resisted when God tried to recruit him. Only after God had given him numerous assurances did Moses confront Pharaoh and demand he release the Jewish people.

And what kind of gratitude did Moses receive from the people? Did they thank him for his efforts? Did they thank him for leading them from Egypt? Not even close!

The people were tired and thirsty from marching through the wilderness of Zin. The blistering sun beat down on their heads. The blasts of desert wind scorched their faces and filled their eyes with dust. Two-and-a-half million thirsty people turned into a hot, sweaty mob. They wanted water. And they wanted it now.

"You have deliberately brought us into this wilderness to get rid of us, along with our flocks and herds," they fumed at Moses. "Why did you ever make us leave Egypt and bring us here to this evil place? Where is the fertile land of wonderful crops—the figs, vines, and pomegranates you told us about? Why, there isn't even water enough to drink!" (Numbers 20:4-5, Living Bible).

Angry at the people but unsure what to do, Moses consulted the Lord. Once before, God had miraculously provided water out of a rock that Moses was told to strike. This time the Lord told Moses to speak to the rock, not strike it. But Moses was too upset. Angrily he called the people a pack of rebels and struck the rock twice with his staff. Water gushed out, but his outburst cost Moses a home in the Promised Land: "Because you did not trust in me enough to honor me as holy in the sight of the Israelites, you will not bring this community into the land I give them," God said (Numbers 20:12).

Depression was another problem for Moses. He once became depressed because he felt inadequate to lead the nation. His attention to detail prevented him from allowing anyone else to offer help; he tried to do everything himself. Eventually he burned out and told the Lord, "I cannot carry all these people by myself; the burden is too heavy for me. If this is how you are going to treat me, put me to death right now—if I have found favor in your eyes—and do not let me face my own ruin" (Numbers 11:14-15).

How did God deal with Moses during his times of anger and depression? Repeatedly God comforted his servant with his presence. He answered his questions with specific answers and gave him support in the form of Aaron and other godly leaders. And at times God disciplined him.

And what of Moses? How did he respond to God's comfort and correction? He learned to flex. He allowed seventy elders to help him govern the nation (Numbers 11:16-17). He stepped out in faith and took daring risks because God commanded him to do so.

Understanding an Idealist

The pessimism of an Idealist tends to make everything look negative. Circumstances appear gray or black.

Don was seized with depression after his initial conversation with the president of the basketball club. He saw himself as a failure, a typical reaction for an Idealist. If you're an Idealist you probably find criticism painful because you believe it means you're either failing or just getting by. Idealists find success hard to come by.[7]

Their Fears

Why do Idealists need to examine every detail before making a decision? Why do they stubbornly cling to familiar methods of living, coaching, or teaching?

Buried beneath their warehouse of facts lurks that familiar fear of exposure and rejection.

Don's father seldom affirmed his son's child-hood efforts. Although Don was an excellent ath-lete in several sports, his dad rarely said, "Good job!" Don always tried his best, but his dad seemed to require perfection. Don was driven to fulfill his father's expectations—but did he ever succeed?

Not quite. And the childhood wounds inflicted by feelings of inadequacy remain buried beneath adult layers of protective armor. The thickest and most visible layer is composed of systems of living which have worked in the past. If a method of coaching or parenting worked before, why give it up and run the risk of failure?

This inflexibility is linked to fear of exposure. An Idealist knows he's imperfect but constantly gathers data to prove that he's okay. Accepting correction is hard because to admit a mistake might call into question his basic worth. Conse-quently, Idealists carefully arrange the facts to prove they're right. If proven wrong, they may become angry, depressed, or both.

Their Inflexibility

It's not terribly helpful for an Idealist to tell himself, "I must be more flexible." He probably knows that already. If you're an Idealist, I suspect by now your spouse and friends have informed you of the fact. Yet when faced with a choice between changing a proven system or keeping it the same, odds are you'll leave it alone (even if it isn't as effective as it once was). Your current method of parenting or coaching gives comfort because it protects you from looking imperfect. At the core of your personality you hate to admit personal flaws. Why? Because while you know you're imperfect, you don't believe you should be.

Don had a terrible time when we tried to get him to say, "I'm not perfect, and it's okay."

"But, Bill," he protested, "It *isn't* okay to be imperfect. I know I'm sinful, but I strive for perfection. I don't want to be the way I am!"

Don is frightened by long, steady gazes inside. He wants to look away. It's hard for him to admit personal flaws without concluding he's totally flawed. A long, inward look overwhelms Don. He deeply wants to be accepted but sees too many ugly spots to believe others could do so. The result? He sinks into a pit of depression.

For an Idealist parent or coach, the safest way to avoid emotional pain is twofold: (1) Avoid looking inward; (2) Try to perform perfectly.

An Effective Idealist

Proven systems of behavior really do diminish the risk of failure; that's why it is so hard for an Idealist to look inward and to be willing to change. Yet, that look and that willingness is crucial if an Idealist is to grow. Idealists must see their own imperfections while keeping them in perspective. Flexibility is impossible until Idealists recognize that God sees both their good and bad points . . . and still accepts them. God saw the "wretchedness" of Moses and yet affirmed and supported him.

Be Flexible with Yourself

Every grade isn't an A+ . . . every team isn't a champion . . . every hitter isn't a Babe Ruth . . . and every parent isn't perfect. God didn't expect perfection from Moses, nor does He expect it from you.

When Moses realized God accepted him, warts and all, he was free to accept the help of other godly men. He could be flexible and take risks. He didn't have to be perfect. God would accept him even if he didn't perform perfectly as the Jewish deliverer.

Idealist parents and coaches—God also accepts you, even when you make mistakes. Mistakes never tarnish his acceptance of you.

Be Flexible with Kids

Nowhere is flexibility more important than in dealing with children. Every child is different and no one system works equally well with each child. Shouting may motivate one child and crush another.

Coaching children requires the wisdom of a fisherman. Flies attract trout in a mountain lake. Herring attracts salmon in the open ocean. No skilled fisherman would ever think of fly fishing from a boat in the open sea. That same kind of wisdom must be shown both at home and on the athletic field.

Don once tried fitting each of his children into a rigid system of study. "It worked great with our first child," he said. "He loved school and never complained about an hour of study each day before and after school. He kept his room clean and lived a structured life."

Don's second child was different, and when he entered school, problems developed. "That kid is disorganized and free-floating," Don said. "Whenever I tried to fit him into my system of study he'd go into his room and listen to his radio."

Don tried strict discipline. He took away his son's radio and restricted him to his room. Nothing worked until Don sat down with his son and helped him devise his own system of study.

Kids need flexibility from parents and coaches. That doesn't mean coaches should hold practices without plans or that parents should allow children to run families. Rather, teaching must be adapted to fit each child. Flexibility is a key to good parenting and coaching.

But the structures of parenting and coaching aren't the only candidates where flexibility is required. Expectations must be flexible, too.

Idealists constantly strive for personal perfection and therefore demand perfection from others. Don was frequently criticized for his "nit-picking" about every detail of the game. At practice Don offered more criticism than praise and became frustrated when the kids failed to perform.

He didn't become more positive with others until he lowered his personal expectations. As he grew in self-awareness, Don relaxed and enjoyed sports activities, even when he didn't play well. The day arrived when he could actually play golf without throwing his club if a drive sliced into the woods. As he lowered his personal expectations, his relationships improved. Slowly, Don began to focus on the positive.

"He still slips into periods of nagging criticism with me and the kids," said Nancy, "but usually it's triggered by a problem at work which has him down on himself. As a family we're sure having more fun."

If you're an Idealist, try to remember that kids play sports to have fun. Learning a skill perfectly is secondary to the pleasure derived from the game. Be flexible with yourself and others and you'll enjoy life more fully.

Be Decisive

Closely linked with an Idealist's resistance to change is reluctance to make quick decisions. Idealist parents want all possible information before coming to a decision. They fear unwise decisions might result from failure to consider every alternative.

The root of the problem once again lies in the fear of exposure and rejection. Nothing is riskier than making a quick decision. What if the decision proves to be wrong?

Indecisiveness was a problem for Moses. God wanted a quick decision. Would Moses agree to enter Egypt, approach the most powerful ruler in the world, and demand the release of 2.5 million slaves? Moses gave God five reasons why he wasn't qualified for the job (Exodus 3:10-4:23). The prophet had no problem listing everything that could go wrong, and he had a hard time deciding whether he would obey God. In fact, he didn't obey until the Lord guaranteed his success.

Don, too, has trouble making important decisions. It took a long time for him to decide whether to propose to Nancy. He sought counsel from every friend he had before he made his decision. Fortunately, Nancy had the patience to hang in there while Don made up his mind.

Nancy has learned that Don avoids making fast decisions, and that reluctance frustrates his kids. If the children want to spend the night with a friend, Don hesitates to give an answer until he's asked every possible question. He's motivated by an almost insatiable need to make the right choice. He knows he's not a perfect parent, but that doesn't stop him from striving for perfection with every decision.

Before a game Don meticulously studies his players. He carefully places each child in the position he believes will strengthen the team. He enjoys the process when he has time to study. But anxiety pounces when key players don't show up and he's forced to quickly decide how to rearrange the lineup. Any coach becomes frustrated when players fail to show, but Don's frustration comes more from having to make a quick decision than from an absent player. A quick change in the game plan might mean a poor performance as coach.

Can indecisiveness be overcome? Yes! God helped Moses by offering him both personal assurances and the help of Aaron. If you're an Idealist coach, try to recruit an assistant who's more intuitive about decision making.

Remember, God doesn't expect perfect decisions, only our best effort. If you have limited time to make a decision, then make the best decision you can and move on. The important thing is to make your choice. Don't drag out a decision while you gather information. If Moses had delayed in confronting Pharaoh, the Jewish people might still be in Egypt. Ultimately, Moses had to decide whether God could be trusted.

Live by Faith

Moses learned that fear could only be conquered as he placed his trust in God. With the Egyptian army attacking his rear and the Waters of the Red Sea lapping in front, Moses found himself caught in a nutcracker squeeze. If his people fought, the Egyptians would crush them. If they moved forward, the Red Sea would swallow them.

Moses, the Idealist, had to make a fast decision. What would he do? God had a simple solution: "Tell the sons of Israel to go forward."

At that moment Moses could have given scores of reasons why the plan might not work. He could have mentioned the absence of lifeguards, the weight of wet clothes, the children who couldn't swim. He could have turned against the people and hammered them for their persistent, rebellious spirit.

But he didn't. Against every one of his natural inclinations Moses cried out, "Stand firm and you will see the deliverance the LORD will bring you today. . . ." (Exodus 14:10-31).

The rest is history. Moses the Idealist, the perfectionist, the conservative, Moses the man afraid of failure—this Moses took a risk and saw the faithfulness of God.

Don, too, has seen God help him overcome fear. Recently he told me how a parent had thanked him for the positive reinforcement he had given his child.

Nancy sees changes at home, too. She sees greater flexibility. "I recently forgot to replace his toothpaste tube and he used mine without a murmur" she said with a wink and a smile, "and he didn't even try to squeeze it 'the right way.'"

ON THE PRACTICE FIELD

1. It's not unusual for you to have feelings of inferiority. God thinks of you otherwise (1 Peter 4:10).

2. Don't hold grudges or save emotional trading stamps (Ephesians 4:26, 27).

3. lt's normal for you to have reservations about an untested plan. God is committed to giving you direction (Philippians 4:6, 7).

4. High commitment to excellence is the positive side of your personality; feelings of impending doom and hopelessness are part of the negative side. Focus on Psalms 91-92 to maintain a proper perspective.

BASIC FEAR: *Being viewed as imperfect.*

KEY VERSE: *". . . and in him you have been made complete"* (Colossians 2:10 NASV).

UNDERSTANDING
YOUR
CHILD

THE GO-GETTER

Strengths

Produces immediate results
Makes quick decisions
Persistent
Problem-solver
Takes charge
Self-reliant
Accepts challenges
Goal-oriented

Ideal environment:

New and varied activities
Continual challenges
Difficult assignments
Autonomy
Control
Direct answers

Weaknesses

Insensitive to others
Impatient
Disregards risks
Inflexible
Unyielding
Takes on too much
Inattentive to detail
Demanding of others

Needs others to encourage:

Sensitivity
Caution
Attention to facts and details

6

The Go-Getter

All Ernie wanted was to help his parents celebrate his mom's birthday. Was it his fault the hospital didn't want her to leave work?

"Do you have any idea how embarrassed I was when my nursing supervisor told me, and the entire nursing staff, what you did?" Jan asked her son. "I would have crawled under the carpet if people hadn't been standing on it. How could you have called the hospital and begged my supervisor to let me stay home? She said you pleaded with her for ten minutes. I can't believe you told her I had been under a lot of pressure and needed time off! It isn't your role to make those kinds of calls!"

My own first encounter with Ernie came when I helped coach his Little League baseball team. One day I was working with the kids on their base running, instructing them about sliding and stealing bases. I stressed the importance of watching the base coach.

"The coach can see the field better than you can, so do what he tells you!" I said.

The next game the boys ran the bases well. All of the boys, except Ernie, followed my instructions. Ernie didn't like me telling him how to run the bases; he felt he could beat the pitcher, catcher, outfielders and anyone else on the other team. My problem, from his perspective, was that I didn't realize his speed and agility.

Some kids won't steal a base unless the baseball is on the other side of the park, and then they almost get picked off because they take so long to take off. And once they're off they may stop to make absolutely sure it's safe.

Not Ernie. If he had a chance to steal a base, he'd go. He often made it, but not always. Occasionally his impatience got him picked off when he failed to wait for a clear opening.

Pitching appealed to Ernie as much as base stealing. He didn't have blazing speed, but he was amazingly accurate. He could place the ball just about anywhere. One day I asked how he learned to throw so well. He smiled and told me he practiced.

"Who catches for you?" I asked.

"Nobody," he answered.

Now, not too many pitchers practice alone, so I asked how he managed without a catcher. Ernie said he had nailed a basket to his house and threw a couple hundred balls at it every day.

"Isn't that kind of hard on your baseballs, not to mention your house?" I probed.

"I don't use baseballs, I throw tennis balls," he said.

Of course! I should have known.

Joseph, the Go-Getter

While the Bible isn't filled with stories of children, some who are mentioned showed their personality styles at an early age. Joseph is seventeen years old when the Bible reveals some of his Go-Getter characteristics.

While no one knows what actually happened around the dinner table when Joseph was a boy, we can make a guess from the facts we do know.

As the family settled down to enjoy a hearty dinner, Joseph, young and handsome, looked at four of his older brothers. "Why didn't you guys watch the sheep more closely? You let them eat the grass all the way down to the ground! (Genesis 37:2).

Joseph showed little concern for his brothers' feelings. He wanted the job done right and he let his father know when it wasn't.

That remark might not have been so provoking if Jacob, Joseph's father, hadn't already made it clear that Joseph was his favorite son. In fact, Jacob had given Joseph a special ornamental robe, and whenever he wore that robe Joseph visibly reminded his brothers that he was numero uno on the family totem pole. Joseph showed little compassion in letting his brothers know he was destined for greatness.

One night he had a dream in which he symbolically saw his brothers bowing down before him. Did he keep the dream to himself? No way! The next day he explained the dream in detail.

Joseph's horrified brothers said, "Do you intend to reign over us? Will you actually rule us?" (Genesis 37:8).

Later Joseph had a similar dream in which both his brothers and parents bowed down before him. Again, he let his brothers know that one day the entire family would serve him.

Clearly, Joseph's dream was from God. God had planted in that teenager a vison of what would one day happen, but in communicating his dream, Joseph failed to consider the feelings of his family.

Go-Getters often need to experience a traumatic event to get their attention. Joseph did when his brothers, filled with hatred, sold him as a slave to a caravan of Midianites who took him to Egypt (Genesis 37:25ff).

During those years in prison, Joseph never forgot the dream. He never gave up on the hope that one day he would be a ruler.

Years later, chastened by God, Joseph became a great leader in Egypt. Eventually, Joseph and his family were reunited, and when he revealed himself to his brothers, Joseph wept. The man who had shown insensitivity by flaunting his destiny had learned that God alone accomplishes His purposes.

Understanding a Go-Getter

Both Ernie and Joseph illustrate the strengths and weaknesses of a Go-Getter. Ernie showed great determination and persistence when he pleaded with his mom's boss to let her off work so she could celebrate her birthday. He showed decisiveness and independence through his base running. He daily practiced pitching a baseball by himself.

And what of Joseph? He was consumed with his own goals. Didn't he give a bad report about his brothers, seemingly to improve their work and win the approval of his father? And he wasted no time in telling his family they would one day serve him.

Their Fears

People like Joseph and Ernie display a self-confidence that can intimidate. Yet oftentimes, when this veneer is stripped away, others are given a glimpse of what's really inside.

Baseball season gave me such an insight into Ernie. Ernie hates to lose. He has a hard time handling a loss, even if the game isn't important. Many times I've seen him cry when his team lost, and I've wondered: Why is losing so painful to Ernie?

There are several reasons. Ernie's mother recently began working, and he hasn't received as much parental attention as did his older brother. His parents shower him with praise whenever he makes a good grade in school or does well in a sporting event, but if he does poorly or if his team loses, they say nothing. No criticism, no praise. Nothing.

Since the fear of losing is built into Ernie's personality, his parents' behavior only reinforces those fears. Ernie's Go-Getter inclination drives him to be aggressive and competitive. Losing is emotionally painful to a child who believes it makes him unacceptable. He may express that pain by crying, fighting, or quitting.

The fear of rejection, which Go-Getter children associate with losing, also helps explain why they tend to be manipulative and insensitive. If winning is the only way to avoid exposure and rejection, doesn't it make sense to disregard the feelings of others who stand in the way of winning? Doesn't it seem reasonable to manipulate others if it will help get wins?

An Effective Go-Getter

Ernie's mother worried about her son's reaction to losing. "I felt pretty good about his competitiveness until the first time his team lost and I saw him crying," Jan said. "The other kids weren't crying. I wondered what was wrong with Ernie."

Jan assured Ernie that losing was no big deal, but he didn't seem to believe it.

"After the first few losses I began to realize I was sending Ernie mixed messages," she added. "I told him losing was okay, but I daily stressed the importance of winning. And I praised his efforts when he won."

Cultivate Security

Anyone prefers winning to losing. But children need to know they are unconditionally accepted. The only way to overcome a Go-Getter's fear of rejection is to stress his value apart from a win/loss record. He must see that his worth is in no way associated with whether he scores a touchdown, throws a strike, kicks a goal, or wins a game.

As a prisoner in an Egyptian jail, Joseph experienced God's unconditional love. God elevated him to a position of responsibility while he was in prison by giving Joseph the ability to interpret dreams.

At a time when Joseph had nothing to offer God except himself, the Lord extended his love. Joseph discovered that God, without human help, would accomplish his purpose, and that included making Joseph a ruler.

His understanding of God's unconditional love and sovereign purpose prompted Joseph to tell his brothers, " . . . You intended to harm me, but God intended it for good to accomplish what is now being done. . . ." (Genesis 50:20). Joseph learned that, regardless of his circumstances, God loved him.

A Go-Getter child should be able to say confidently, "Neither a bad grade, nor a fielding error, nor a missed tackle, nor a strike out, nor any other loss shall be able to separate me from the love of God." And they should also know that nothing, absolutely nothing, can ever separate them from the love of mom and dad. Such confidence enables Go-Getters to face their fears. It enables them to try their hardest to win without being devastated by a loss.

Parents can communicate such love by taking advantage of teachable moments. Perhaps in the evening, just before your child goes to sleep, you could tuck him or her into bed and talk about the day. Reassure them of your love. Those little slices of time nourish children with a sense of security and well being.

Give your children jobs and allow them to fail without criticism. Let them mow the lawn, even if they chop it up. Allow them to prepare a meal, even if they burn it. Play board games and stress the fun of playing more than the pleasure of victory.

Never, ever, compare children. Nothing creates a fear of failure more quickly than the suspicion that parents are measuring one child's mental and physical abilities against another's.

Cultivate Sensitivity

Result-oriented, Go-Getter children aren't motivated by a sense of compassion. To ask Ernie, "How do you think Mike felt after you refused to pass him the football when he was wide open?" won't have much affect. Ernie doesn't care how Mike felt. He wants to win!

Is it possible for a child like Ernie to put the needs of others before his own? Certainly, but it will require patience and perseverance on the part of both parents. As a Go-Getter's sense of personal security grows he'll be more open to considering the needs of others.

While parents must demonstrate unconditional love, they must also teach their children to act unselfishly even when they don't feel like it.

A child like Ernie will question the wisdom of putting others first. Ernie's parents must help him realize that the only way Mike, and the team, will improve is through practice. If Ernie holds the ball nobody else will improve. When a man is open—any man—he must make the pass. Furthermore, if he refuses to pass, it's time for a little visit on the bench.

Helping a Go-Getter child make choices based on what's best for the team, however, isn't the same as developing compassion. Real compassion involves emotions, feelings of genuine concern for others. Go-Getter children can be encouraged into such feelings by linking them into the emotions of others.

How can that be done? First, the parents of a Go-Getter need to pray daily that God will cultivate a heart of compassion in their child. The apostle Paul was so transformed by God that he once wrote: "I speak the truth in Christ—I am not lying, my conscience confirms it in the Holy Spirit—I have great sorrow and unceasing anguish in my heart. For I could wish that I myself were cursed and cut off from Christ for the sake of my brothers, those of my own race'' (Romans 9:1-3).

Paul changed because of the Holy Spirit's transforming power. Parents need to pray for such a change in their children.

But they must do more than pray. Sensitivity develops by encouraging children to listen to others. Parents of Go-Getters must create an environment where others are heard out. Go-Getters have fixed ideas about most subjects so they often don't listen; but they can't be allowed to get by with that. At home and at practices, help them develop listening skills. Teach them to ask questions. Help them rephrase what they have heard and repeat it to the speaker.

There's probably no better time to practice such skills than at the dinner table. Why not devote an evening meal to developing family listening habits? Have one family member describe a recent disappointment. Next, encourage each child to ask a question about what happened, then summarize what they heard. Such practice will help everyone become better listeners. Listening allows us to hear another's needs.

Finally, developing compassion in a Go-Getter requires a new focus, a higher goal than winning a game or making an A in school. They must learn that when we please Christ, we win in the game of life. In 1 Corinthians 10:31 Paul said that we are to '' . . . do it all for the glory of God.'' Parents need daily to remind their children to please Christ and bring glory to God. That's not natural for any of us, but it can be cultivated. Once cultivated, it allows a Go-Getter to think about something other than winning or losing.

Develop Patience

A Go-Getter's drive to win can make him unfeeling and impatient. Once when Jan was flat on her back with two herniated discs, Ernie pleaded with her to take him *right now* to a discount store to buy baseball cards.

"Mom, please," he begged, "I need to get those baseball cards; they'll be gone if I don't hurry."

"Ernie, I can hardly get out of bed."

"Well, call a friend or someone," Ernie insisted.

"When your dad gets home he'll help you."

"But he won't be home until after the store's closed!"

Ernie wanted those cards. He wanted them fast. Motivated by a sense of urgency he called several of his mother's friends and asked if they would please take him to get the cards.

Go-Getter children need to develop a willingness to delay gratification. That may mean allowing them to make impulsive decisions so they can suffer the consequences. On other occasions it may mean urging them to save for a future purchase. On the athletic field it may mean learning skills they see no reason for developing.

Give a Challenge

Most of what I've said about Go-Getters involves helping them to slow down and develop gentleness. But what if they're discouraged? How can they be challenged to reach for a higher goal when they're down?

An experience with Andy illustrates the kind of challenge that encourages a Go-Getter.

Somehow Andy became terrified of batting. Each time a pitched ball sped his way, Andy stepped away from the plate. All a pitcher had to do was throw strikes and Andy would be out.

For weeks the coach stood behind the backstop screaming at Andy to "stay at the plate; don't back away!" Andy, an excellent athlete, felt humiliated and angry.

One day before a game I sat next to him and asked, "Are you afraid of the pitcher?"

"No way!" he replied.

"Are you afraid of many kids at school?"

"No!"

"Andy, did you know that when you step up to the plate to bat, it isn't a contest between you and the ball, but between you and the pitcher?"

"I hadn't thought about it."

"When you back away from the plate the pitcher thinks you're afraid of him; so do his teammates."

"Well, I'm not afraid of that guy."

"Oh yeah," I said, "then prove it to me the next time you bat."

I wish I could say this approach works with every Go-Getter. It doesn't. But from that day forward,

Andy stood in the batter's box and hit the ball. He became one of the best hitters on the team.

Go-Getters love a challenge. They function best in an environment which offers challenge, freedom, and variety. When restricted they'll rebel just to demonstrate their autonomy. But since they're so self-confident they eagerly respond to a challenge.

Ernie's mom ended up having a back operation. From her hospital bed Jan told stories of her son's perseverance and determination. With a broad smile she said, "Yes, there's never a dull moment around our house; Ernie sees to that. He's sure fun to have as a child. But, Oh! What a challenge!"

Chances are if you have a Go-Getter child, you're smiling right now and saying "Amen."

ON THE PRACTICE FIELD

Working with a Go-Getter:

1. Go-Getters are goal-oriented and sometimes make decisions that cause them to step over existing boundaries.

2. Go-Getters fear loss of control and can sometimes respond in an aggressive manner to remove opposition and regain control.

3. To encourage change you must confront their actions, but never their character or integrity.

4. When confronting a Go-Getter, be short, direct, and to the point.

5. Because Go-Getters have high ego needs, they may prefer to discuss different alternatives with a third party. The loving thing to do is to provide the opportunity.

6. Allow time and the Holy Spirit to communicate the message.

BASIC FEAR: *Being viewed as a loser.*

KEY VERSE: *"Whoever wants to become great among you must be your servant, and whoever wants to be first must be your slave"* (Matthew 20:26).

THE PERSUADER

Strengths

Optimistic
Enthusiastic
Personable
Makes a favorable impression
Articulate
Desires to help others
Entertaining

Ideal environment:

Friendly atmosphere
Freedom from detail
Opportunity to influence
Public recognition
Opportunity to talk
Excitement about ideas

Weaknesses

Lacks follow-through
Oversells
Overestimates results
Misjudges capabilities
Acts impulsively
Jumps to conclusions
Overcommits

Needs others to provide:

Follow-through
A logical approach
Concentration on a task

7

The Persuader

While Cindy prepared lunch in the kitchen, I stretched out on the couch in our den to watch television. I enjoy those quiet moments alone with the TV.

Suddenly the back door banged open. Two waist-high kids exploded into the room, skidding to a halt the moment they saw me.

"What is it?" I asked, jumping up.

The ashen face of David, my middle son, told me something was up.

"I'm afraid to tell you!" David said.

"Come on David, tell me what happened."

David swallowed hard, glanced at his friend Jenny, looked back at me, and whispered, "I threw a rock through our neighbor's window."

"You did? Why would you do that?"

"Well . . . I wanted to show Jenny what would happen."

"Didn't you know the window would break?"

"It was just a little rock! I thought it would bounce off."

"And what did you learn?"

Jenny tossed her brown curls and announced, "He learned that if you throw a rock at a window it'll break."

This rock episode wasn't the first time David had gone out of his way to impress his friends. During one soccer practice I told the boys to stand beside their balls and get ready to learn a new move.

"I already know how to do that!" David declared.

"Are you sure?" I asked.

"You bet!"

"Okay, show the team how to do it."

David, an excellent player capable of some tricky moves, rolled his left foot over the ball and hopped with his right foot. Then he got stuck. He repeated the moves but couldn't remember what to do next.

After a frustrating moment he looked up and said, "Well . . . I could do it before."

And he probably could.

David works hard on perfecting unusual moves. When the two of us practice alone he often wants to learn some soccer trick he saw on television. During a game he'll actually try the move. It might not work, but he's not afraid to take risks and try something unusual—especially if his friends find it entertaining.

At times, David's need for social recognition creates trouble. Several years ago when I picked up David from soccer practice his coach told me he hadn't been paying attention at practices.

"He's been kinda rowdy. Stirs up the other boys. I'm not sure how to handle him," the coach explained.

Later in the evening as David slipped on his pajamas I asked how practice went. "Fine," he replied. He had enjoyed himself.

"Any problems?" I asked.

"I don't remember any." He walked over to his desk and picked up a baseball card.

"Do you remember being rowdy?" I persisted.

"Not really," he said, "but this is a cool baseball card."

I could tell David wanted to end our discussion and snuggle with our Cocker Spaniel. Serious conversations make him nervous.

"David, don't you remember your coach getting upset because you were being rowdy?"

"I guess so; but the other guys were acting up, too!"

"I believe that, but let's deal with you. What did you do?"

David gazed at me with his hazel eyes and slowly admitted, "I guess the coach got mad at me for throwing water on the other guys during the water break."

"David, what's more important, having fun with your friends or obeying the coach?"

"Obeying the coach," he replied.

"Have you noticed that when you're with your friends you sometimes do wrong things to get them to laugh and have fun?"

He nodded, "Sometimes I do."

"How should you act in those situations?"

"I should do what's right. Even if the other kids are being rowdy."

"What would have been right today?"

"I should have obeyed the coach and not played around with the other guys."

"What will you do the next time?"

"I'll try to listen to the coach and obey him."

Some kids crave candy, others want toys, but a Persuader child loves being around friends. Spending time with other kids actually recharges their emotional batteries, and other kids love being around them because they're fun and funny. Persuader children, like David, generate excitement and enthusiasm.[8] Kids like David will participate in almost any activity which gives them social strokes, and they'll avoid those which deny them recognition.

Jonathan the Persuader

If any young man in the Old Testament illustrates the personality of a Persuader, it has to be Jonathan. Consider the scene described in 1 Samuel 13-14.

Armed with iron swords and spears, the Philistines had assembled three thousand chariots and six thousand horsemen to wage war against King Saul and his small army (1 Samuel 13:5). The only Israelites with iron swords were Saul and his son Jonathan. Humanly speaking, the Israelites didn't have a chance.

Early one morning Jonathan spoke secretly with his armor bearer, "Come, let's go over to the Philistine outpost . . ." (1 Samuel 14:1b). The two snuck out of the Israeli camp and found a garrison of twenty Philistines.

Jonathan told his armor bearer they would reveal themselves to the Philistines. If the enemy asked them to come up to them, the two would attack. Jonathan's logic was simple. He figured if the Philistines asked them into their camp then ". . . the LORD has given them into our hands." And the armor bearer was persuaded, "Do all that you have in mind . . . I am with you heart and soul" (1 Samuel 14:7).

Without thought for his life, Jonathan attacked the Philistines and defeated them. When word of the victory spread to the enemy camp, the Philistines trembled.

Jonathan had great ability to lead and encourage others. He was willing to take an enormous risk which defied reason, and he couldn't imagine losing a battle if the Lord was with him.

Later, Jonathan's boldness turned to disrespect and led to trouble. King Saul had forbidden the army from eating any food on the day of an important battle. But on seeing some honey, Jonathan filled his mouth with the sweet food.

When some of the men in the army told Jonathan about his father's restriction, he avoided responsiblity for his actions. He said, "That's ridiculous! A command like that only hurts us. See how much better I feel now that I have eaten this little bit of honey" (1 Samuel 14:29 Living Bible). Jonathan even said that his father's restriction had prevented the Israelites from routing the Philistines.

Once the king's son had shown disrespect, it was easy for the rest of the army to rebel. Later in the day, after a victory over the Philistines, they violated the Mosaic law by killing some livestock and eating the meat with blood in it (1 Samuel 14:32; Leviticus 17:10-14).

Jonathan used his Persuader boldness and verbal skills to blame his father for his own wrong doing, which set the stage for others to disobey God.

How did the Lord deal with another classic Persuader? Consider the apostle Peter. He couldn't imagine ever denying the Lord. But he did . . . three times.

After the resurrection, Jesus met with Peter alone. Just the two of them. I've often wondered what Jesus said. Nobody knows what the two discussed, but I'd guess Jesus wanted to reassure Peter of his love. In spite of Peter's denial, the Lord loved him.

How did Christ's unconditional love affect Peter? On the day of Pentecost, Peter preached and three thousand Jews accepted Christ as their Savior. Peter, the impulsive Persuader who had abandoned Jesus, was transformed by Christ's love into a bold spokesman.

Understanding a Persuader

Persuader children have a lot in common with Jonathan and Peter. They have an "I can do it" attitude. David thought he could teach his team a new soccer move. Jonathan believed he and his armor bearer could defeat a garrison of Philistines. Peter thought he would confess Jesus rather than deny him.

Such optimism often causes Persuaders to oversell their abilities. They believe they already know how to hit a baseball, field a grounder, catch a fly, mow the lawn, do a math problem, or cook a meal.

Persuaders also love excitement. Consequently they sometimes act before thinking. David unthinkingly threw a rock through a neighbor's window.

A Persuader's love of excitement may occasionally land him into trouble, as when David's rowdiness angered his coach.

Their Fears

David likes good feelings—excitement—and he may act up to create that excitement. I have to take the time to talk through problems with him, to pointedly encourage introspection. He doesn't do it naturally. Introspection exposes weaknesses, causes negative feelings, and can be unpleasant.[9]

When David does look inward, it hurts. It forces him to deal with why he misbehaves at school or practice. He has to discover why he tends to be unrealistic in viewing his own abilities. As a parent, I need to listen carefully so I can discern his inner motivations.

Talking with David has led me to believe that Persuader children, like people of other personality types, fear exposure and rejection. The crucial question is, what do they fear others might see?

The answer flows from understanding how much a Persuader craves acceptance. Persuaders want to be the life of the party. Often their need for the latest toy or designer clothes reveals an immense need for acceptance. They hope that an outer facade of laughter and good looks will conceal an inner fear that they aren't likeable or attractive. They fear rejection if their inner weakness and ugliness were to be exposed.

Easily Directed

That deep, inner fear may cause Persuader children to lose control over their actions. Like a tree branch swept away by a mountain stream, Persuaders are easily influenced by their friends. Surrounded by rowdy kids, a Persuader will become the loudest child in the group. Directed by peer pressure, a Persuader can easily become "cliqueish." They may dress, talk, and walk in ways calculated to impress the group. Meanwhile, concerned parents may stand aghast by their child's increasing drive to please friends.

What happens when a parent confronts a Persuader about improper behavior? Usually they'll shift blame onto someone or something else. David acted surprised that the "little rock" had shattered the neighbor's glass; it was the other members of his soccer team who first acted rowdy.

How can parents help Persuader children grow through their weaknesses?

An Effective Persuader

It's imperative that we deal with our children in the same way Jesus dealt with Peter. Jesus' private, post-resurrection meeting with Peter was not to condemn or embarrass. Likewise, confronting Persuader children with their mistakes must be done in a non-threatening environment. The last thing a Persuader wants is for a friend to see his flaws.

Offer Love

Persuaders are more likely to listen to correction in the context of love and acceptance. They need to know that parents and coaches accept them in spite of bad behavior. Only as they realize they are already loved will a Persuader be free from an insatiable need to win love through entertaining behavior. When Peter realized Jesus loved him, he found the freedom he needed to preach boldly to the Jews. John said, " . . . perfect love drives out fear . . ." (1 John 4:18b).

Parents and coaches must never forget that love drives away fear. When children are secure in their parents' love they are less likely to try and earn the acceptance of their peers through bad behavior.

Even in the context of acceptance, however, a Persuader may avoid taking responsibility for improper actions. In that case, we must do what Jesus did with Peter: We must force them to deal with their behavior.

As Jesus and Peter walked alone along a rocky beach, Peter asked the Lord about his plans for John. The Lord told Peter it was none of his business. His business was to follow Jesus (John 21:22b). We, too, must force Persuader children to deal with their own attitudes and actions.

Stand Alone

It's tough for Persuaders to do what's right when their friends are doing wrong. Real tough! But they must learn to do just that.

Serious discussions and repeated failures help Persuaders learn. As they grow secure in their relationship with God and their parents, they'll be able to stand alone. Proverbs 1:10-19 talks about the importance of standing alone and not getting swept along by the crowd. Many times I've read that passage to David, trying to help him realize the danger of misbehaving to please others.

David's episode with dousing his soccer team buddies called for discipline. He needed to learn the importance of standing alone; that's why I didn't allow him to play with his friends after school for three days. Few things motivate a Persuader child like his desire to be with friends.

A wise parent or coach can use this as a teaching tool. At practice, a rowdy Persuader can be sent off by himself to do individual drills until he's ready to cooperate with the rest of the team. Around the house a Persuader shouldn't be allowed to play with friends until his homework and household chores are done. On other appropriate occasions, have them write out what they did wrong and how their attitudes and behavior should change. The practice of sitting alone and writing forces introspection—something they don't normally do.

Follow-Through

Excellence in athletics, as in life, requires discipline and follow-through. Few ever became skilled at a sport without daily practice. Persuaders like to have fun with friends, and disciplined behavior often evades their grasp.

Some time ago Cindy asked David to do the dishes. Around our house, doing the dishes includes cleaning the rest of the kitchen. When she later surveyed his work she found the dishes clean, but the rest of the kitchen in a mess.

"David, weren't you supposed to do the dishes?" Cindy asked.

"Yes," he replied.

"Son, you haven't finished doing the dishes until the entire kitchen is cleaned up."

"Oh! I didn't know that."

Starting is easy for a Persuader, finishing isn't. Athletics provide an excellent place for kids to learn discipline and follow-through. On the soccer field David's a good forward. He likes to beat defenders and kick goals. Persuader children have a passion to score because they love the applause of the crowd. They are good finishers in soccer and runners in football.

But on defense they take it easy. Who ever applauds a defender?

"David, you're not going to play forward for a while," I announced at one practice.

"Why not?" he asked.

"Because I want you to learn to defend. When you show as much hustle on defense as you do on offense, I'll move you back to an offensive position."

That's life. We can't just give it our all when circumstances are going well and we're having fun.

The Bible makes it clear that much of life is made up of trusting God in tough times.

Persuaders need parents who insist on clean rooms even when friends aren't coming over. They need parents who don't consider daily chores completed until they're completely finished, parents who don't think homework is good enough until it's as good as it can be.

Certainly nobody's perfect. And who wants a prison for a home? But Persuaders need structure to learn follow-through. Otherwise, they'll become lazy, and later in life they'll suffer for it.

Think before Acting

Coaches can design drills which require players to think, to make choices. Parents can help their children to consider beforehand the alternatives and consequences of their actions. Persuaders must be allowed to make impulsive choices so they can learn the danger involved.

For several months I told David a bedtime story about a great white bird. At moments of crisis the bird, visible only to the boy, would land on the hero's shoulder and whisper in his ear: "Think before you act!"

Night after night the tale took the boy through burning deserts and across raging rivers. A single, impulsive decision would result in certain death.

I treasure one moment at bedtime when David rolled onto his side and prayed, "Lord, help me learn to think before I act. Help me want to please you more than my friends."

A little boy's nighttime prayer—that's all. Or was it?

I don't know. But I do know David is beginning to realize his weaknesses and to bring them before God. He's learning it's important to admit his failures and to ask God to help him overcome them.

I'm glad I heard that prayer. And I'm glad I'll see God's answer.

ON THE PRACTICE FIELD

Working with a Persuader:

1. When confronting a Persuader, be aware that they may use their verbal skills to manipulate the facts.

2. Recognize that Persuaders have an overly optimistic view of their abilities and the abilities of others.

3. Be aware of the a Persuader's need for flexibility.

4. When correcting a Persuader, build a friendly, accepting environment.

5. Show Persuaders how to accomplish their job, and be aware of a Persuader's need for recognition.

BASIC FEAR: *Being viewed as unsuccessful.*

KEY VERSE: *"Whatever you do, work at it with all your heart, as working for the Lord, not for men, since you know that you will receive an inheritance from the Lord as a reward. It is the Lord Christ you are serving"* (Colossians 3:23-24).

THE SPECIALIST

Strengths	**Weaknesses**
Supportive	Resists change
Agreeable	Difficulty with deadlines
Loyal	Overly tolerant
Self-controlled	Indecisive
Consistent	Holds grudges
Good listener	Possessive
Performs set work patterns well	Lacks initiative

Ideal environment:	**Needs others to encourage:**
Appreciation	Risk-taking
Freedom from conflict	Facing difficulty
Security	Self-motivation
Affirmation for a job well done	
Limited responsibility	
Stable relationships	

8

The Specialist

The old gym at Hunt Junior High looks like a big box. Its old wooden floor carries the scars of high-heeled shoes, metal chairs set up for assemblies, and kids playing basketball in street shoes. Thick, gray curtains shield tall windows from flying balls.

Junior high kids have scratched hearts, initials, and dates on the brick walls. Tan paint covers the messages, but the impressions remain. The gym now stands empty, carrying like a tomb the memories of school days past.

I first visited the gym on a day it throbbed with life, filled with shouting girls, bouncing balls, and the shrill of a referee's whistle. The gym almost seemed to breathe.

A team in red advanced the ball across half court. Quickly I spotted Cara, her short, blond hair overshadowing a light sprinkling of freckles on her upturned nose.

Cara received a crisp pass and dribbled up the far side of the gym past two defenders.

"Shoot!" yelled Andy, her coach.

She passed the ball to a teammate who lofted it toward the basket. The ball hit the backboard and ricocheted off the rim into the outstretched hands of an opposing player.

Shortly thereafter the game ended and I spoke with John, Cara's dad.

"What did you think of our team?" he asked. Even though John is less than six feet tall, he played basketball in college. He's one of those former athletes who's still in shape. His thick brown hair and broad smile cause him to look young for his age.

"You know, I don't know why Cara won't shoot the ball," he continued without waiting for my answer. "She's our best player, but since about our third game she hardly ever takes a shot. We're still winning, but I'd like to know why she won't shoot."

"Why don't you ask her?" I suggested.

"I have, but I didn't find out much," John replied. "Maybe I'll give it another try."

A few days later John called to give me an update on his conversation with Cara.

"Bill, you're not going to believe this," he said. "Cara wasn't shooting because during the third game, after she missed a shot, her coach called a time out and told her not to shoot again without making at least two passes. She wasn't shooting because that's what she thought he wanted."

This wasn't the first instance when Cara's sensitivity to others showed up.

Cara loved basketball and practiced shooting several hours a day—she knew her dad played ball and she wanted to please him. He showed her how to shoot and would occasionally play one-on-one with her. By the time she played on a team she was best player in her age group.

Another time, after failing to make an honors science team, Cara became despondent. Her good grades started slipping, and one of her teachers, Mrs. Higgs, became concerned. Hoping to encourage her, Mrs. Higgs urged Cara to study harder; but instead she became withdrawn and slothful.

Mrs. Higgs didn't give up. She met with Cara and asked her to become a lab assistant for the science team, a position created just for Cara. Cara recorded the results of the team's work, and Mrs. Higgs praised her efforts. The more affirmation Cara received, the more she blossomed. The extra attention transformed her. She started listening in school and her work soon improved.

Cara, like other Specialists, values relationships. She's motivated more by a desire to please those she loves than by a love for winning or making A's. Once she does decide to try something, however, she'll work hard to perfect her skills.

Samuel the Specialist

Samuel was probably ten years old when he assisted Eli the priest in the house of the Lord.[10] At a time when God rarely revealed Himself through visions or words, God audibly spoke to young Samuel.

Alone in the temple, Samuel found a comfortable place and stretched out to rest. Suddenly he heard a voice: "Samuel!" Immediately he sat up and looked around. Thinking it was Eli, he jumped to his feet and ran to his master.

Surprised that Samuel had awakened him, the priest told his young helper that he hadn't called. He then urged Samuel to return to bed.

Again Samuel lay down to sleep. Once more he heard someone call out: "Samuel!" Believing that Eli had summoned him, Samuel again rushed to his master. Eli assured young Samuel that he hadn't called. After the voice called Samuel a third time, Eli told Samuel that God was calling him and he should listen for a message.

"Samuel, Samuel!" the voice cried out a fourth time. With wide eyes and wildly pounding heart, Samuel said, "Speak, for your servant is listening."

From that moment on, Samuel's life would never be the same. God told Samuel that he intended to destroy Eli's family because of their sins.

The next morning Samuel faced a major crisis. Eli wanted to know what God had told him. Eli had been a father to Samuel for over seven years; the last thing Samuel wanted to do was pass on such painful news.

Eli gently urged Samuel to speak; then he pleaded with him. Finally, he asked the Lord to judge them both if Samuel didn't tell him everything (1 Samuel 3:17). Only after such urging did Samuel freely share all that the Lord had told him.

Specialists tend to be peacemakers. They value smooth personal relationships over everything else, and at times their agreeable spirit may cause them to bend over backwards in pursuit of peace. When tension exists between themselves and others they may expeience unbearable pain. That's why Samuel was so reluctant to tell Eli what the Lord had spoken to him.

Years after God first spoke with Samuel, when he served as a prophet and priest, he had to inform King Saul that his crown would be removed and given to another. Samuel became so distressed that he cried out to the Lord for an entire night.

Later, we find that after informing Saul of his impending removal from the throne, Samuel never saw Saul again. Why? Because "Samuel mourned for him" (1 Samuel 15:35b). He loved Saul and was grieved over this one God had rejected as ruler over Israel.

From an early age, Samuel placed his relationship with God above all human relationships, and throughout his life the strength of his walk with God enabled peacemaker Samuel to make tough decisions and deliver tough messages.

Understanding a Specialist

Specialists aren't driven as much by a passion to win as by a desire to please those they respect. That's why Cara worked harder in school after her teacher strengthened their relationship. That's why, after her coach told her not to shoot without first making two passes, she refused to take any shots.

At times, a Specialist's need to have peaceful relationships may cause them to compromise their moral convictions. Had Samuel not developed such an intimate walk with God, it would have been easy for him to overlook some of King Saul's sinful behavior.

Specialists take pride in their work. Whatever they do, they want to do well. Samuel performed his roles of priest and prophet with great proficiency. Under his leadership schools were established to train young prophets, the rightful worship of God was renewed, and the nation of Israel increased in military strength. A similar commitment to excellence could be seen in Cara as she diligently practiced to improve her game.

Their Fears

Because Specialists are such peaceful children, their worries are seldom apparent. Parents usually assume everything is okay and they fail to probe beneath the surface. Many parents find it hard to believe that a Specialist often hides behind this peaceful behavior. What are they afraid of?

Specialist children feel weak and inadequate. They fear others will see their weakness and despise them.

As long as no tension exists in their relationships, Specialists feel safe, but the slightest indication of tension stirs up fear. Specialists try to make peace to relieve that fear.

It's not that Specialists won't argue, but they may withdraw from an angry parent in the middle of an argument, or lie to avoid conflict.

In an effort to appear strong and effective, they'll practice hard so they can perform their specialty well. They hope a good grade in school, a touchdown, or a homerun will cause others—especially those they admire—to respect them. They want to please their parents, coaches, and friends.

But what happens when they don't make the science team? What happens when their layer of protection is shattered by failure? What happens when others see their imperfections?

How do Specialists respond when their efforts to make peace fail? What happens when they feel alienated from parents, coaches, or friends? How do they handle the deterioration of a relationship even though they tried to make peace?

When Specialists hurt, they either try harder or else they withdraw.

What can parents do to prevent a Specialist child from withdrawing? If a Specialist has hidden in an emotional cocoon, what can a parent do to draw him out? How can the parents of a Specialist help their child become more assertive in the face of possible rejection?

An Effective Specialist

God's dealing with Samuel gives us a perfect model. Samuel repeatedly faced difficulties. At times he had to impart painful news to friends. On other occasions he had to stand up to national leaders. Such situations would be tough for anyone. For a Specialist they would seem unbearable.

How did God prepare Samuel for such hardships? Early on, God made himself known to Samuel. When he was only ten years old, Samuel learned that anywhere he went God would go with him. He discovered that obedience to God would bring a blessing.

Offer Love

Specialists need to know that both God and their parents love them. They must know they are loved in spite of their weaknesses. Neither poor performances in school or bad showings in athletics must be allowed to weaken that confidence.

Only as Specialists experience such love will they be able to handle tension in personal relationships. Knowing the love of both God and their parents will give a Specialist the security needed to disagree with others without feeling like a failure.

Coaches of Specialists need to remember that these children value relationships above winning. Taking the time to develop a friendship with them will make them more coachable.

Cultivate Faith

As Specialist children come to believe that God will protect them, they won't have to hide behind a protective layer of perfect performances and peaceful relationships. They'll do what they know to be right, trusting God to take care of their friendships.

Parents can help their children cultivate such faith by urging them to express their feelings—even if they disagree with a parent, teacher, or coach. Specialists need affirmation when they confront others or become assertive.

John made it a point in his talk with Cara to urge her to speak to her coach about why she refused to shoot. The last thing Cara wanted was to tell her coach why she wasn't taking any shots.

"What are you afraid of?" John asked.

"He'll think I'm silly or crazy," Cara stammered.

"Are you?"

"Well, no," she whispered, looking at her feet.

"Come here, Hon," John said.

Reluctantly, Cara approached her dad. John wrapped his arms around her and gently gave her a hug.

"Hey—there's nothing silly about your feelings. You wanted to please your coach. That's okay! I see why you felt that way. But now you need to tell him why you weren't shooting."

The two talked some more and then John prayed with his daughter about what she'd say to her coach.

Cara faced her fear of rejection head-on that day. The result? She grew a bit more confident and assertive.

Explanations

Specialists need to process what they're told. A careful and logical explanation will often help overcome their fear of failure.

John once assumed Cara resisted learning new basketball moves because she thought she didn't need his help. He remembers the first time he took an extra moment to explain why he was teaching her a new move. Her eyes lit up and she said: "Oh! Now I see what you mean!" In a flash she wanted to learn all she could.

Clear Demonstrations

Specialists need hands-on instruction more than most other children. Their fear of performing poorly is overcome by demonstrating what's expected of them.

Cara, like other Specialists, likes to have a parent or coach show her exactly what to do.

A Persuader child doesn't wait for a demonstration. He's so sure he can do whatever is asked that he'll try anything. A Thinker child will weigh the information to see if it seems safe.

A Specialist, on the other hand, wants to make sure he doesn't appear foolish by performing poorly. He'll wait for a clear demonstration to show exactly what's expected. Then, and only then, will he give it a try.

Specialists need to learn that it's okay to take a risk, even if it means they may not look like an expert.

Later in the basketball season I paid another visit to the old gym at Hunt Junior High. Again Cara brought the ball across the court. But this time when she had an open shot she took it. I smiled as the arching ball swooshed through net without touching the rim.

ON THE PRACTICE FIELD

Working with a Specialist:

1. Whenever a change affects the family of a Specialist, be sure and allow them time to adjust.

2. Whenever they are being taught something, be supportive of their efforts.

3. Specialists fear confrontation and they avoid conflict. They need your support when they are confronted and when they need to confront.

4. Continue to define and clarify goals and objectives for a Specialist. Use pictures, drawings, or actual hands-on demonstration to explain what's expected of them.

5. Reinforce the message each time a Specialist makes progress toward his or her goal. Specialists possess an innate need for security and assurances.

6. Read over the story of Abraham (Genesis 12-25). Note his tendency to avoid conflict. How did God help him learn to trust Him in the face of adversity? Help your child think about the character of God and why He can be trusted during times of personal conflict.

7. Help your child learn to work faster and initiate more. Help him plan out a practice strategy for his favorite sport or activity.

BASIC FEAR: *Being viewed as weak and inferior.*

KEY VERSE: *"For you created my inmost being; you knit me together in my mother's womb. I praise you because I am fearfully and wonderfully made"* (Psalm 139:13-14a).

THE THINKER

Strengths

Orderly
Conscientious
Disciplined
Precise
Thorough
Diplomatic
Analytical

Weaknesses

Indecisive
Overattention to detail
Rigid
Avoids conflict
Hesitant to try new things
Avoids full responsibility
Pessimistic

Ideal environment:

Detail-oriented
Stable surroundings
Reassurance and affirmation
Clear understanding of expectations
Time for planning
Commitment to quality

Needs others to encourage:

Decision-making behavior
Self-confidence
Optimistic point of view

9

The Thinker

Why wasn't my son doing his best? The other boys were playing hard—what was wrong with Ryan?

"Come on Ryan!" I yelled. "Hustle!"

"It's no use," he yelled back, "I can't keep up with him. He's too fast!"

"Well, try anyway!"

Our team consisted of fifteen All-Star boys selected from the Lake Oswego Soccer Club. We played against teams a year older than us in order to develop our players. The boy Ryan was supposed to guard towered over him a full head and shoulders.

Ryan dropped his head and walked along the sideline of the soccer field, discouraged. That was too much; I'd had enough. I yanked him out of the game, hoping a few minutes on the bench would teach him a lesson.

I was wrong. He sat on the ground a few feet from the playing field, dejected and beaten.

The older team dominated us for some time. Finally we scored. Our players leaped into the air and celebrated: "Hey! We can beat these guys!"

I glanced at Ryan, hoping that the excitement of the score would bring him to his feet. It didn't. He just sat with a blank look on his face, offering neither support nor praise.

Frustration, embarrassment, and anger boiled inside me. That kid sure knew how to make me mad!

In spite of the noise on the playing field, my thoughts shifted to the first time I attended one of Ryan's practices. I had expected to see a chip off the old block, a boy aggressively fighting his way through the other kids. Instead he watched the game from a distance. He ran, but took few chances.

That's why I pushed him. We practiced. We worked. I pushed some more. Hadn't such tactics worked with me? Sure, he despised it, but I continued anyway.

I got angry after one of those miserable practices in which I forced Ryan to run through "boring" drills. Without a word I picked up the orange practice cones and stomped toward the car. Dead silence clasped hands with mean feelings. Real mean!

Tears streamed down Ryan's freckled face as we approached our home.

"What's wrong?" I asked.

"You didn't talk to me all the way home," he sniffled.

At once a rush of love and compassion—and guilt—filled my heart. I stopped the car, embraced my son, and assured him of my love. I asked him to forgive my insensitivity.

Suddenly, shouting on the field interrupted my stroll down memory lane. I glanced at Ryan sitting on the ground. Many times other coaches had told me, "Ryan's an excellent player with great ball skills, but he has to be more aggressive."

I knew for certain that many of my past efforts to help Ryan had failed. I wanted to encourage my son, but I wasn't sure how.

As the first half came to a close Ryan got off the ground and began to show some interest in playing. I started him in the second half and he did a great job. To our surprise, we won. We beat the older team!

On the drive home Ryan sat silently beside me in the front seat.

"Son," I asked, "what happened out there today?"

"I don't know," he replied. "The guy was bigger than me and so I gave up. I don't know why."

"Son, do you realize you're going to face a lot of bigger and faster players?"

"I guess so."

"Ryan, I want you to know that I love you whether or not you beat your man. I love you even if our team loses. But what will happen in your life if you give up when faced with stiff opposition?"

"I don't know. I guess I won't accomplish much."

"Does the Lord care if you win or lose?"

"No."

"What does He want from you?"

"He wants me to do my best."

Understanding a Thinker

Lots of children are like my oldest boy. Thinkers tend to move to the side of the field. They seem best at watching. Most of their parents aren't sure if they should shout or be quiet.

How do you help a Thinker? One of the best ways is to understand a few of their basic personality traits.

Perfectionistic

Thinkers are fundamentally perfectionistic. Ryan's annual search for the perfect pumpkin illustrates that trait.

Each October our family visits Wilhelm Farm, a tiny ranch set atop a small hill fifteen minutes south of our home. We get our choice of thousands of pumpkins—oval ones, round ones, big ones, small ones. Every size and almost any shape.

Every family member picks out a pumpkin. Later we each draw faces and carve out jack-o'-lanterns.

It takes about thirty minutes for Cindy, David, Paul, and I to select our pumpkins. And what about Ryan? He's examining every pumpkin in the patch. He's got to pick *the* best one; nothing less than perfect for Ryan. Finally he finds just the right one. Everyone rejoices that finally we can go home. But wait, Ryan has a question: "Dad, do you think the one I just spotted is better or the one I picked before?"

Such perfectionism creates unrealistic pressure on the field of competition; no athlete is perfect. No gymnast scores only tens. No runner wins every race. No baseball player bats 1.000.

Cautious

This compulsion to do things the "right way" makes Thinkers cautious. Children like Ryan often would rather give up than do something below their high standards. Parental exhortations to "do better" or "try harder" seem to fall on deaf ears.

Indeed, such words may have the opposite effect. Rather than hustling, thinkers might become withdrawn. Why? Because they have a hard time believing they're okay if their actions are imperfect. Their reasoning is simple: No risks taken, no failures possible.

Feelings like that can paralyze an athlete. There isn't time on the field to gather data and take the safest route. Players must learn to act intuitively, and that's not easy for a thinker.

Sensitive

A Thinker's extreme desire to avoid mistakes creates great sensitivity. They cherish safety and security. They need to know they are loved. Beneath their desire for all the facts lies a deep need for security.[11]

Thinkers don't want to take any chances until all information is gathered and evaluated. Their self-worth is directly tied to their performance. If they don't perform well, they feel like failures. Criticism may be painful because the slightest flaw means failure, and failure means rejection.

An Effective Thinker

Perfectionistic and cautious, Esther was a Thinker. While both Moses and Luke fit the Idealist/Thinker pattern as adults, Esther showed the traits as a young girl. Though she was only a teenager, the future of thousands of Jewish people rested on her shoulders. And to make matters worse, she had to act quickly.

Esther never dreamed she would become the queen of Persia. She no doubt wondered how it could have happened. Only a few years before, both her mother and father had died. Fortunately, her older cousin, Mordecai, raised her as his own daughter.

She probably would have married a Jewish man if the king's servants had not noticed her beauty. One day she was just another Jewish teenager living in exile in Persia. The next day she was brought to the palace and groomed for the position of queen. When she stood before King Xerxes, after a year of cosmetics, fine food, and the best of servants, her beauty melted the king's heart.

But her fairy tale soon turned into a nightmare. One day, a servant told Esther that Mordecai, her adoptive father, sat in sackcloth and ashes before the gate of the palace.

Esther sent the servant to talk with Mordecai and find out why he was fasting. The servant returned and told her that an enemy of the Jewish people had persuaded the king to kill every Jew in the kingdom. Mordecai pleaded with her through the servant to beg the king not to kill her people.

Immediately Esther saw everything which could go wrong. If the king found out she was a Jew, he might kill her. And, according to the king's law, if she or anyone entered the king's presence without first being summoned, he might kill that person.

Like Moses, who years before had told God all the reasons why he couldn't confront Pharoah, Esther sent a message to Mordecai letting him know that her speaking to the king wasn't such a great idea.

How did Mordecai respond? Did he rebuke her cowardice? Did he tell her to "Grow up!" On the contrary, he gave her the information she needed as a Thinker. He told her if she didn't act, her family would die, but God would raise up someone else to save the nation. He encouraged her with a reminder that perhaps she had been elevated to royalty for this very purpose (Esther 4:13, 14).

But Esther needed one last assurance. She asked Mordecai to have all the Jews fast for three days. Given that assurance, she approached the king. Although just a teenager, she saw God use her to deliver the Jewish people.

Unconditional Love

Thinkers need answers to their questions. They must be given assurances. They need to consciously realize that all God wants from them is their best effort. That's all . . . just their best effort. Obviously, that may mean they'll never be a super star. And, we who are parents must accept and reward our kids when they do their best, even if they aren't exceptional athletes.

If we say "God only wants your best," but we show disappointment over their performance, what are we communicating? Aren't we telling them their best isn't good enough?

Correct thinking begins with an awareness that God and parents are pleased with effort even when the results aren't always base hits or touchdowns.

Faith in God

After Mordecai assured Esther he and the rest of the Jewish people would fast, she put her trust in God (Esther 4:16). She had to act. She had to take a chance. With the king before her and the threat of death behind her, she moved into the king's presence.

God proved himself faithful. But Esther had to take a risk to see his faithfulness.

Similarly, our children need to have their faith

stretched by the games they play. A fielded grounder, a caught fly, a good defensive play, an open field tackle—all provide Thinkers with opportunities to see the faithfulness of God enabling them to do their best.

Ryan and I learned that his passivity could be overcome with cool reasoning and assurances. His goal after that first game was to try his best, even if he didn't see any chance of winning. He made a commitment to play aggressively, regardless of how he might feel.

Almost a full season after Ryan had first struggled against an older, bigger opponent, he got another chance in Round Two. The team facing us was big, fast, intimidating—the same team we faced in our first game.

The shrill sound of the official's whistle filled the air. Our boys controlled the ball, brought it up the side of the field, shot, and missed. Our opponents reversed the field and unsuccessfully attacked our goal.

As our team passed the ball across the midline, Ryan trotted by me, smiled, and said, "I can beat him, Dad!" It was the same boy Ryan had given up against earlier in the year.

I remembered that first game and smiled. Oh, I knew there'd be other games, bigger opponents. Times of discouragement would come. But in that moment I savored the character I saw growing in my son. In that instant I knew he had won a big one.

ON THE PRACTICE FIELD

Working with a Thinker:

1. Thinkers want clearly identified areas of responsibility. Any changes require personal assurances, accurate data, and an exact description of where they fit into the big picture.

2. Expect questions for clarification and answer them directly. Use non-threatening voice tones and neutral body language. Provide as much detail and as many reassurances as you possibly can.

3. Thinkers have unrealistic expectations which frequently cause them to feel sorry for themselves and give up without trying.

4. Given time to reflect, a loving environment, and a third party to act as a sounding board, Thinkers will frequently turn 180 degrees from their negative position. They will often need to ask the third party to approve of their thoughts or actions so they can move forward.

5. Thinkers may need to be led by the hand until their confidence increases.

BASIC FEAR: *Being viewed as imperfect.*

KEY VERSE: *"There is now no condemnation for those who are in Christ Jesus, because through Christ Jesus the law of the Spirit of life set me free from the law of sin and death"*
(Romans 8:1).

PLAYING
THE
GAME

10

Real Champions

Eric was born with dwarf legs and an extra big toe on each foot. When his umbilical cord was cut, it only had two arteries, indicating kidney problems.

Eric was a day old when the doctor told Gary and Caron Warddrip that their son had a bilateral inguinal hernia, a hernia that ran from hip to hip. He also had a severely dislocated hip. He was placed in an ankle cast and harness to straighten out his legs, but months later it was apparent the cast and harness hadn't helped.

When Eric was several months old he had hip reduction surgery. Later he would have two more operations on his hip, three on his hernia, one on his esophagus, two on his legs, and one on his feet.

"We thought we had things under control until we moved to New Mexico," Caron said. "Once at the higher elevation Eric had trouble breathing. The doctors did a battery of tests and determined he had a hole in his heart. During a blizzard we drove him to Denver for open heart surgery."

In spite of Eric's physical limitations, Gary and Caron were determined to give him as many experiences as possible.

"We included him in everything," Caron said. "We adopted the verse which says, 'I can do all things through Him who strengthens me' (Philippians 4:13). 'Can do!' became our philosophy and approach to life with Eric. After his heart operation we went on a boat trip in Utah. Eric, hooked up to oxygen tanks, went with us. He had a great time. I think he learned to play sports because we concentrated on what he could do rather than what he couldn't do."

Play sports? That's right. While many people might consider Eric Warddrip the last person to play any kind of sports, play sports he did. The first time I spotted Eric trotting onto the soccer field he flashed a big smile, brushed a hand through his brown hair, and kicked a ball to a friend. He walked with a slight limp, but who could have imagined the hardships he had endured to get him to that point?

Understanding Disabled Children

The way Caron and Gary handled Eric showed great wisdom. Their methods were later affirmed by Brad Bafaro, an educational specialist who works with disabled children in Forest Grove, Oregon. Brad received the 1987 Teacher of the Year award from the Oregon Association of Retarded Citizens and is well-equipped to speak knowledgeably about the experience of disabled kids.

"To begin with," Brad said, "I never use the word *handicap* when referring to children who suffer from a mental or physical disability. And I never call kids without such limitations normal. After all, who's really normal? Every child has some kind of limitation. Parents and children don't need to worry about disabled kids getting hurt any more than they worry about anyone else getting hurt. All children run the risk of an injury when they play sports. A parent, coach, or teacher has to take the time to know the kid he's working with."

Access Skills

That knowledge, Bafaro says, starts with discovering what a disabled child can do. Once that's determined, allow the child to participate at a level where he can experience success. Let him play, but do it in a way that doesn't spoil the game for others.

When Eric first started practicing with our soccer team, I knew nothing about his many surgeries or his close calls with death. I saw a cheerful boy who walked with a limp and stood shoulder height to the other players. After looking more closely, I noticed red scars on his legs. Still, he could run and kick a ball just fine; his only limitations seemed to be speed and strength.

Eventually I played him at a defensive position where he wouldn't have to cover as much ground. He was successful at that position and contributed to the team.

Our other players realized Eric's limitations and gave him help when he needed it, just as they did for any other player. Every member of a team has strengths and weaknesses and needs the rest of the team to be successful.

Assess the Sport

In many ways Brad Bafaro stands in sharp contrast to the children he teaches. As a gymnast he picked up sports quickly. His strong hands can hold and swing a baseball bat with power and control. His legs carry him with speed and agility. He can play almost any sport with a high level of proficiency.

But for Brad, being the best hitter, fastest runner, or strongest kicker isn't the aim of a sport. He wants the children he teaches to play in such a way as to develop skill and get a taste of success.

"You must know enough about the sport to see where the child can find success," Brad counsels. "For instance, Jerry is a paraplegic. He has full use of his arms and can throw, catch, and hit a baseball, but he can't run. He played pitcher for a while but couldn't get out of the way of hard-hit balls. I ended up playing him at catcher. He did a super job catching the ball from his wheelchair.

"In working with disabled kids, the game must be broken down into smaller pieces. Their progress may be much slower, but they'll progress—and that's what gives them and their coach a sense of accomplishment. With kids who have a hard time hitting a baseball, I allow the pitcher to stand closer than normal. Once they can hit consistently at one distance, I have the pitcher move farther away. The idea is to help the kids develop their athletic skills, to stretch them."

Eric's dad applied this second principal beautifully. Eric had always wanted to play basketball, so Gary bought him a ball and put up a backboard, securing the hoop at six feet instead of the usual ten. Gary figured Eric would play for a few days and then tire out . . . but he didn't. Eric came home from school and practiced basketball two hours a day. Eventually Gary had to raise the basketball rim to ten feet because Eric was getting so good.

Encourage Success

Disabled kids need to be encouraged by allowing them to succeed and then presenting them with new challenges.

"Working with disabled children just takes more patience," Bafaro says. "It requires a new definition of success which isn't measured by winning but by learning and improving a skill such as hitting a baseball or kicking a soccer ball."

That's the way Jack Snook, Eric's basketball coach, dealt with Eric. Jack discovered what Eric could do on the basketball floor and designed a play to help him score points. Game after game Eric lofted the ball toward the basket and saw it swish through the net. As Eric rejoiced in his success his teammates slapped him on the back and offered their congratulations.

Isn't it fortunate that God deals with each of our disabilities in a similar manner? He evaluates our abilities and then gives us opportunities to spread our wings. Luke 10:1-16 tells how Jesus sent the seventy before him in pairs to the villages where he would soon minister. Later, the seventy returned to the Lord rejoicing and said, "Lord, even the demons submit to us in your name" (Luke 10:17). Jesus used that moment of success to further instruct the seventy concerning their future ministries.

Thousands of years earlier, the Lord commanded Moses to confront Pharoah. The shepherd trembled with fear at such a thought. To encourage him the Lord had Moses toss his staff on the ground. Immediately it became a writhing snake. That success bolstered Moses's confidence and enabled him to move forward (Exodus 4:1-4).

Involvement

A disabled child won't learn a sport if a parent sits in an armchair and watches. Parents must work with their children.

The Warddrips learned early on that doctors can mend bodies but not hearts. Right away they decided to do everything possible to help Eric reach his full potential. When he lived in the cocoon of a body cast, they made a special table with a harness so that he could sit up and look around. Later they made him a special tricycle so that he could do what other kids his age did. They evaluated his skills at each stage and devoted themselves to his success.

Remember God's Purpose

Where does God fit into such a scheme? The same day I heard of Eric's surgeries and hospital stays I asked Eric himself how he felt about all his difficulties.

"I thought everyone had tough times," he answered. "I'm just glad God made me like He did."

"Could I look at your feet?" I asked.

"You'd like to see my feet? No kidding? Sure, I'd be glad to show you my feet!"

As he took off his high-top tennis shoes Caron explained how hard it was finding shoes for him. Eric requires a different size for each foot.

"Here they are, Bill. What do you think?"

I choked back tears as I gazed at his feet.

"Here's where they removed the toe," Eric said, pointing at a spot on the outside of his foot. "And here's where they took the bone for my ankle," rubbing his hand over scars on both legs.

My, I thought, *this Eric is a true champion!* He can dribble with confidence down a basketball court and make an assist on a goal. He can bring a soccer ball across a field. But until I saw his feet I didn't understand what a champion he really was. Eric had overcome more obstacles than any child I had ever coached. He had overcome fear of failure and rejection. He had overcome pain, repeated pain.

His parents had a lot to do with that. They always focused on what he could do. They concentrated on what he could become even when the doctors said, "It's in God's hands . . . we don't know if he'll live," even when the social worker said, "If I were you, I'd have him institutionalized."

Through all of that the Warddrips believed God had a higher purpose for their son. They continually looked to God for the strength needed to work with Eric.

"Working with disabled children just takes more patience," Brad Bafaro would say. "It requires a new definition of success which isn't measured by winning but by learning and improving a skill."

Eric's tortured feet remind me of what Brad knows so well: kids like Eric are real champions.

ON THE PRACTICE FIELD

1. If you coach or parent a disabled child, ask God for the grace to cultivate a "can do" attitude in the child.

2. Help the child select a sport. Work with him to determine what he can do, and patiently help him develop his athletic skills.

3. If, as a coach, you're reluctant to work with a disabled child, meet with the parents and find out what the child can do. Try to gain information to help you overcome your fears so that you can offer the child an opportunity to succeed.

4. If you struggle with why God allowed you to parent such a child, read over Psalm 139. You might examine some of the magazines and organizations included below.

The following organizations, listed alphabetically, can provide information about local, national, and international programs for disabled athletes.

American Athletic Association of the Deaf
3916 Latern Drive
Silver Springs, MD 20902

American Blind Bowler's Association
150 North Bellaire
Louisville, KY 40206

American Wheelchair Bowling Association
6718 Pinehurst Drive
Evansville, IN 47711

Amputee Sports Association
11705 Mercy Boulevard
Savannah, GA 31406

Canadian Wheelchair Sports Association
333 River Road
Ottawa, Ontario, Canada

Disabled Sportsmen of America, Inc.
P.O. Box 26
Vinton, VA 24179

International Council on
Therapeutic Ice Skating Association
P.O. Box 13
State College, PA 16801

Joni and Friends
P.O. Box 3333
Agoura Hills, CA 91301
(818) 707-5664
(A Christian organization formed for the purpose of addressing the needs of the disabled).

National Association of Sports for Cerebral Palsy
1701 K Street, N.W.
66 East 34th Street
New York, NY 10016

National Beep Baseball Association
3212 Tomahawk
Lawrence, KS, 66044

National Foundation of Wheelchair Tennis
3857 Birch Street, Suite 411
Newport Beach, CA 92260

National Handicapped Sports and Recreation Association
Capital Hill Station
P.O. Box 18664
Denver, CO 80218

National Wheelchair Athletic Association
2107 Templeton Gap Road, Suite C
Colorado Springs, CO 80907

National Wheelchair Basketball Association
110 Seaton Building
University of Kentucky
Lexington, KY 40506

National Wheelchair Marathon
Hill Road
Warwick, RI 02886

National Wheelchair Softball Association
P.O. Box 737
Sioux Falls, SD 57101

North American Riding for the Handicapped
Box 100
Ashburn, VA 22011

Special Olympics
1701 K Street, N.W.
Suite 203
Washington, D.C. 20006

United States Association for Blind Athletes
55 West California Avenue
Beach Haven Park, NJ 08008

Magazines for Disabled Athletes

Palaestra
Challenge Publications Ltd.
P.O. Box 508
Macomb, IL 61455

Sports 'N Spokes
5201 N. 19th Ave., Suite 111
Phoenix, AZ 85015

For further insight into current research on sports and disabled individuals, see:

Appenzeller, H., *The Right to Participate: The Law and Individuals with Handicapping Conditions in Physical Education and Sports* (Charlottesville, Va.: The Michie Co., 1983).

DePauw, K., "Research on Sports for Athletes with Disabilities," *Adapted Physical Activity Quarterly,* 3 (1986): 292-99.

Sherrill, C. ed., *Sports and Disabled Athletes* (Champaign, Ill.: Human Kinetics, 1986).

Sherrill, C., *Adapted Physical Education and Recreation: A Multidisciplinary Approach,* 3d ed. (Dubuque, Iowa: Wm. C. Brown Co., 1986).

—————— 11 ——————

Superstars

Having a goal can nudge even the most unlikely of kids toward superstardom. Gary Smalley gives such an example in his book, *The Key to Your Child's Heart.*

San Francisco, 1957. A tall, skinny ten-year-old schemed how to sneak inside Kaiser Stadium. All year he had waited for this game between the San Francisco '49ers and the Cleveland Browns. It represented his one chance to see his idol, Jim Brown, the all-pro running back who held almost every rushing record in the NFL.

The boy knew he could slip in when the gate guard left at the end of the third quarter, but even then it wouldn't be easy. Ghetto life had taken its toll on the boy; malnutrition made his legs weak and bowed and he had trouble walking. He needed steel splints just to get around.

Even so he made his way into the stadium and stood right in the middle of the entrance to the players' tunnel. There he patiently waited for the game to end. As the final gun went off, the wiry lad struggled to stand tall so he wouldn't miss his moment. At last he saw Brown turn the corner and walk toward him. The boy held out a piece of paper and politely asked his idol for an autograph. Brown graciously signed it, then turned for the locker room.

Before he could get away the boy tugged on his jersey and proudly confessed, "Mr. Brown, I have your picture on my wall. My family can't afford a TV set, but I watch you on the neighbor's set every chance I get. I know what your records are and I think you're the greatest. You're my idol."

Brown put his hand on the boy's shoulder and thanked him before heading to the locker room. But the boy reached up and tugged Brown's jersey again. Brown turned and looked into the boy's big brown eyes and asked impatiently, "Yes?"

The boy cleared his throat and said matter-of-factly, "Mr. Brown, one day I'm going to break every one of your records."

Brown was taken aback.

"What's your name, son?" he asked.

"Orenthal James, sir," the boy answered, "but my friends just call me O.J."

In 1973, O.J. Simpson broke Brown's long-standing single season NFL rushing record and became the first player to gain more than two thousand yards rushing in one year. He was second behind Brown in yardage when injuries forced him to retire.[12]

No doubt many influences led to the greatness of O.J. Simpson. But few probably influenced him more than a belief that he could break Jim Brown's records. Early in life he set that goal and pursued it vigorously.

Most children need encouragement with goals. For the athletically gifted child, it's crucial for parents to provide direction and support.

Understand Parental Responsibilities

Organized sports is often a part of growing up, and for athletically talented kids it can become almost central. I'm sure that most parents believe unusual athletic ability is a great advantage, yet gifted children sometimes find that the ease with which they pick up sports can work against them. If talented kids don't develop personal goals and self-discipline, they may be surpassed by harder working athletes with less natural ability.[13] And parents who don't learn how to control young superstars may wake up one day to find that their kids don't listen any more.

That's exactly what happened with Samson.

What Bruce Jenner or Carl Lewis are to track and field in the United States, Samson was to the people of ancient Israel. If he lived today his chiseled face would adorn the cover of a Wheaties cereal box. He would be the *Sports Illustrated* Athlete of the Year.

Samson could have played any position in pro football. In Judges 14:5ff we find Samson walking through a vineyard when he spots a lion. The great cat roared and leaped toward Samson, but the man didn't run away or try to hide. Instead he grabbed the cat's jaws and ripped them apart as easily as if the cat were a rag doll. I'd like to see Samson wearing the blue and silver of the Dallas Cowboys. Running backs would think twice before heading in his direction.

Samson was fast, too. He could outrun the fastest Olympic track star. In Judges 15:4 he wanted revenge on some Philistines who had treated him with contempt. He chased down 300 foxes and tied their tails together. He then placed a torch between their tails and released them in the grain fields of his enemies. A man has to be pretty fast to run down three hundred foxes!

Samson also would have made an awesome tennis star. In Judges 15:9ff the Philistines retaliated for Samson's fox stunt by sending their army against Judah. The fearful Judahites persuaded Samson to be bound so they might hand him over to the Philistines. Samson waited until an opportune time, broke the ropes, picked up the jawbone of an ass, and with the flick of his wrist slaughtered one thousand Philistines. Now, that's a wicked backhand!

He was also intelligent. He judged Israel for twenty years (Judges 15:20), and it requires great wisdom to govern a nation peacefully for that long. Especially in the Middle East!

But above all, Samson loved God. From childhood his greatest passion was to serve the Lord. God told his mother that Samson would be a Nazarite from the time of his conception. As a devoted servant of God, a Nazarite couldn't drink alcoholic beverages, eat unclean foods, touch a dead body, or cut his hair. Normally, the Nazarite vow was taken for a short time. But Samson's mother showed a deep commitment to God and her son by keeping the vow during her pregnancy. Samson himself obeyed the vow from the time of his birth.

Samson had it all—strength, intelligence, position, good looks, and a heart for God. In every respect he was a true superstar. He had everything you or I would admire and want for ourselves or our children.

And yet a single weakness led to his downfall; one flaw caused him to forfeit all he valued: His relationship with God, his strength, his vision, his position, all lost. Everything. How did it happen?

A distortion in his personality went uncorrected. Samson himself carries the ultimate responsibility for his actions, but I think we can say his parents share in the blame.

The first recorded words of Samson give his parents instruction about a woman who caught his eye: "I have seen a Philistine woman in Timnah; now get her for me as my wife" (Judges 14:2).

Samson didn't waste words. Upon seeing an attractive woman, he wanted her. He wanted her now! Surely both Samson and his parents knew the prohibition against marrying foreign women.

His parents did put up some resistance: "His father and mother replied, 'Isn't there an acceptable woman among your relatives or among all our people? Must you go to the uncircumcised Philistines to get a wife?' " (Judges 14:3).

Unfortunately, it wasn't enough. Samson insisted on his own way: "Get her for me. She's the right one for me" (Judges 14:3b).

What do you think they did? They traveled to Timnah with Samson where their son married a Philistine (Judges 14:5, 10).

But why did Samson's parents tolerate and even participate in their son's rebellion? Perhaps they felt it was too late to resist his demands. Samson was a young man and a superstar; who were they to stand in his way? Maybe they had so consistently caved in to his demands that they had forgotten how to say "No!"

Whatever the reason, one question lingers: What could they have done differently? In terms relevant to today: How can parents of gifted athletes avoid the mistakes of Samson's parents? How can they help their children develop character and athletic skill without forfeiting their future?

God had already given the Israelites instruction aimed at protecting their children from the evils of the Canaanites. Note the words of Moses in Deuteronomy 6:4-7:

Hear, O Israel: The LORD our God, the LORD is one. Love the LORD your God with all your heart and with all your soul and with all your strength. These commandments that I give you today are to be upon your hearts. Impress them on your children. Talk about them when you sit at home and when you walk along the road, when you lie down and when you get up.

Spiritual Zeal

All coaching begins with the coach. All parenting begins with the parent. That's why Moses exhorted parents to love God with everything they had. Such devotion demands diligence. If we hope to infect our children with a genuine love for God, we must first have the disease. Parents must be spiritual pacesetters.

Our children will follow our example, whether good or bad. They will adopt our values. The major moral decisions they make will be shaped by the values they learn from mom and dad. If we love cars, houses, clothes, money, or sports, so will they. If we love winning more than playing well, so will they. And if we follow God unreservedly, chances are they will, too.

Behavioral studies repeatedly emphasize the importance of role models. Children learn more by observing what their parents do than by what they preach. Young lives are shaped more by family practices than by parental beliefs.[14]

We need to cultivate the kind of spiritual vigor we want our children to copy. That means both dads and moms must be spiritually active.

Spiritual Instruction

Firecrackers are illegal in the state of Oregon. Yet every year around the fourth of July my boys beg for firecrackers. The louder and more powerful they are, the more they like them.

"But dad," they plead, "we can drive over to Washington to buy firecrackers. All of our friends buy them."

The local law seems smart for most people because they don't know how to safely light firecrackers. I do. And I confess I like doing it. So why not buy them?

Violating such laws may seem insignificant, but our attitude toward authority isn't insignificant. If I illegally shoot off firecrackers, am I not modeling for my kids that we can pick and choose the laws we obey? Am I not passing judgment on the right of governmental authorities to outlaw certain dangerous practices? Doesn't that attitude carry over to other authority figures like coaches?

Talented athletes may choose to skip practices because team rules don't apply to good players. They may smoke grass or sniff coke because the laws prohibiting them are "stupid."

Jim McGee, director of psychology at Sheppard Pratt Hospital in Baltimore and a former consulting psychologist for the baseball Orioles, observed that the superb physical endowments of elite athletes may contribute to their problems by making them prone to superman delusions. They may come to believe they are immune to the dangers of carousing, booze, and drugs that strike down lesser men.[15] Parents have the unique opportunity to help their children develop the kind of godly character that can protect them from such dangers.

At mealtime and bedtime Cindy and I often speak with the boys about how the Lord takes care of us. Each evening we review with them the Bible verses they are learning. When issues arise—like illegal firecrackers—we discuss the implications of the decisions we make. Real life situations provide the best classroom for instruction.

Cultivate a Teachable Attitude

According to Gwilym S. Brown in *Sports Illustrated*, Kyle Rote, Jr., was " . . . a genuine, home-grown, 100% American Superstar . . . an ideal choice to lead a new wave of American soccer heroes. . . ."[16] TV fans may remember Kyle as a three-time winner of the Superstars competition. Soccer fans remember him as the 1973 Rookie of the Year and scoring champion when he played with the Dallas Tornadoes.

Kyle didn't begin playing soccer until the age of sixteen and then only to stay in shape during the summer. After a year of football at Oklahoma State, he transferred to the University of the South at Sewanee, Tennessee, where he played soccer. Subsequently he played the game professionally and on the U.S. National Team which represented our country against some of the greatest soccer teams in the world.

Kyle believed the professional scouts hired him, not because of his unusual athletic abilities, but for another reason. He said:

> I think one of the most positive things I had going those first few weeks was not my physical ability, but being able to sacrifice whatever pride I had and say, "Look, guys, I can learn something from every one of you, if you'll help me." I was amazed at how these players—men whom I admired and respected—went out of their way to help me sharpen my skills and teach me the fundamentals of professional soccer . . . I would try to pick out a player each practice to spend maybe fifteen minutes with me after practice that day.[17]

Teachability has to be among the most valuable character traits parents and coaches can build into talented athletes. Few situations reveal the teachability of a child like athletics. A gifted child may feel he can't learn from a coach. He may think he already has all the skills he needs. It's imperative that parents and coaches help such children discover the importance of teachability.

Resistance to new ideas or techniques calls for dialogue. Don't allow disrespect to go by without correction. Children must realize that character only grows in those who are teachable.

Stimulate a Challenging Goal

Athletes must continually be challenged to new heights. Without the challenge of learning a new skill or of mastering a new area of development, the game stops being fun. It's wise for parents and coaches to help their children develop both long- and short-range goals.

Gifted athletes may learn to coast through life because they learn sports so quickly. They may falsely assume that the rest of life will be equally simple.

Each summer I try to practice soccer daily with my three boys. We talk about why we practice and thus review the concept of personal discipline. Each boy has a skill he wants to sharpen; perhaps it's to perfect one new move or to strengthen a kick. The advantage of setting short-range goals is that at the end of the summer each boy can look back with a sense of accomplishment. My role is to make practice fun even as we develop the skills they want to sharpen.

A parent might challenge a basketball player to sink nine out of ten jump shots from fifteen feet out. The parent of a soccer player might encourage a child to learn two moves a year. Such specific, short range goals help an athlete stretch his or her skills.

Long-range goals may include playing a sport professionally or in college. Perhaps making the high school team would be enough of a challenge for certain children. Regardless of the goal, parents and coaches need to help children arrive at goals they will eagerly own. Parents shouldn't superimpose their own goals on a child, but once the goal is stated, parents should help their children achieve those goals.

Spiritual Goals

"To be the best professional athlete I can be is a high goal," wrote Kyle Rote, Jr. in his book, "but beyond that goal there is a higher one—to have a day-by-day relationship with Him who provides depth, meaning, and direction for my life."[18]

Sports become the most fun when our goal isn't to win, but to know the Lord and to do our best for him. Children need parents to help them understand and strive for spiritual goals.

Colossians 3:23 says, "Whatever you do, work at it with all your heart, as working for the Lord, not for men, since you know that you will receive an inheritance from the Lord as a reward."

Parents and coaches must remember that when a child's playing days are over, the character they've developed through athletics will remain. Their relationship with the Lord will influence their professional careers for a lifetime. It's crucial to have spiritual goals that reach beyond the field of competition.

At times we may feel we've failed. Many folks think the story of Samson ended tragically. Because of his sordid affair with Delilah, Samson had his eyes gouged out and was made a Philistine slave. His last act was to pull down the palace of the Philistines, killing all their leaders.

But his story didn't end on a tragic note. After sinning he realized his folly. Baldheaded and blind, he renewed his commitment to the Lord. Slowly, both his hair and relationship with the

Lord began to grow, and the Lord gave him one last, great spiritual victory.

His story both warns and encourages me. It warns me of the dangers of tolerating evil in myself or in my children. It encourages me by insisting that God's grace must ultimately intervene on behalf of all parents. God's grace prevailed in Samson's case despite foolish choices.

And that makes me wonder: Could it be that the greatest gift we can give our children, in addition to our love, is our prayers?

ON THE PRACTICE FIELD

1. As a parent, evaluate your personal walk with God. Are you modeling godly behavior for your children? Be honest with yourself. If you know of areas which need to change, talk to the Lord about your struggle and renew your commitment to personal growth. Remember, children learn more from our actions than words.

2. Most Christian book stores have some great teaching materials. Browse around in one and look for a devotional book or Bible memory plan you can use with your child. Begin praying with your child daily as you implement your teaching plan.

12

Competition

Screaming parents strained their necks to see the game clock, an ancient, orange time piece with big, black minute and second hands.

Less than a half minute remained and the basketball game was tied. It looked like the final shot would decide the league championship. The kids seemed pretty cool, but their parents were going nuts.

When the second hand reached the twenty-second mark the Cougar coach yelled for a time-out. Perspiration drenched his hair, face, and shirt.

This coach meant business. He pointed a finger at one player and then another. The two boys nodded their heads to indicate they understood his orders.

With a shout of confidence the Cougars broke their huddle and hustled onto the basketball court.

A Cougar pass inbounds was intercepted by an alert Eagle who drove down court for an easy lay-up. The buzzer sounded and the parents of the Eagle players swarmed onto the floor to congratulate their kids.

Suddenly, all 6 feet 4 inches and 260 pounds of the Cougar coach erupted into a fit of rage. Kicking an aluminum folding chair halfway across the court, he screamed at the Eagle coach, "You guys cheated!" The chair crashed to the floor at the same moment the coach's words filled every corner of the gym. The next instant, everyone stopped talking. The gym was as quiet as a graveyard. Then, as though someone had turned the sound back on, all the noise returned.

The worst part of the noise came from the mouths of the Cougar players. Following their coach's example, they accused the Eagles of being a "bunch of dirty cheaters."

You may wonder for what title the boys were playing. Surely, an important championship prompted such an emotional outburst—right? Wrong.

Those boys weren't playing for a high school title. They weren't even playing for a junior high title. Those kids were second graders playing for the championship of a youth league.

It's easy to hear such stories and shake your head in disgust. But just wait 'til it's your kid standing at the plate. Then the situation takes on meaning, doesn't it? I know I've caught myself, on more than one occasion, challenging an umpire's call. Obviously, most of us have greater patience when the game doesn't count. But a bad call in a championship game can stoke our fires.

Competition. It's as American as apple pie. Social psychologist Elliott Aronson has noted that, "The American mind in particular has been trained to equate success with victory, to equate doing well with beating someone."[19]

The competitive spirit which drives us may prevent us from enjoying the success of others, even other children. It may cause us to push our kids too hard. It may cause us to give the impression that winning is everything and mistakes are unacceptable. That's probably why some kids weep after losing an important game or making an error.

I'm sure you've felt the tension between a drive to win and a need to be gracious. You've probably wondered "How can I teach my children to be competitive in sports without being obsessed with winning? How can I urge them to try their hardest while letting them know mistakes are a part of life?"

In case you think there's an easy solution to the problem, consider this: after three-and-a-half years with Jesus, his disciples still struggled with an overly competitive spirit.

Look to Jesus

The tiny pebbles and small white shells of the Galilean beach crunched under the feet of the two men as they walked beside one another. Behind them, at a distance, followed a third.

Jesus asked Peter several questions . . . stinging questions. Three times He asked the fisherman if he loved Him. And three times Peter assured the Lord of his love. Peter remembered denying the Lord three times. On the beach he confessed his love three times.

Jesus forgave Peter and instructed him to feed His sheep. Peter would spend the rest of his life obeying that command.

As the Lord spoke, Peter couldn't keep from glancing over his shoulder. Behind them followed John. He always did that. Like a little brother he always wanted to be close to Jesus, even when Jesus spoke privately with others.

Peter heard the command of the Lord but he wondered about one thing. He had a single question that couldn't wait. Peter stopped, looked over his shoulder at John and asked, "Lord, what about him?" (John 21:21).

Peter had to know what Jesus would do with John. While he fed the Lord's sheep what would

John do? Would he build a massive following or humbly serve Peter?

The ugliness of Peter's competitive spirit stained that page of history. But the response of the Lord gives us an effective antidote for obsessive competitiveness.

"Jesus answered, 'If I want him to remain alive until I return, what is that to you? You must follow Me'" (John 21:22). In other words, the Lord said, "Don't worry about my plans for John. Just concentrate on Me."

Our concern should center around our own performance, not the performance of others. We must focus on the Lord rather than on our competitors. Pleasing him should be our motivation and satisfaction.

At practice and in games our drive should be to please the Lord by doing our best. We win when our best efforts are superior to our opponent's; but from the Lord's perspective, we win each time we do our best and seek to please him, regardless of the score.

Now, I'll be the first to confess that such an attitude doesn't come naturally. It requires looking to the Lord and asking the question, "What would Jesus do? How would He act?"

I'm a Producer personality type. I'm driven to win. Yet I've found that when I consciously ask those questions, I'm freed to enjoy competitive sports even in a loss.

Jesus spent years of his ministry trying to teach his disciples to avoid competition by looking to him. His example helps us understand what should be our deepest motivation.

Be a Servant

Servanthood didn't come easily for the disciples. They believed a winner owned many servants. A loser owned none, or served others himself.

They knew the Lord had watched them for over three years. They believed he would pick a leader from among them, a team captain. Each of them wanted to be the greatest.

They thought the Lord sought a general who could dominate, command others, direct servants. They repeatedly tried to demonstrate their ability to control the other disciples so that Jesus would pick one dominant disciple to be his right-hand man.

Never would a disciple be caught serving another. Might not the Lord intepret such behavior as a desire to be a servant? And couldn't that result in a permanent demotion to servanthood?

Imagine the scene. Outside, clear night skies and cold air. Inside, a warm room prepared for a feast. Roasted lamb and baked bread waited on the tables.

Just then the sounds of sandals slapping against the stairs and deep, gravelly male voices interrupted the quiet. The wooden door swung open and the aroma of roasted lamb filled the room. Tired and famished, the men looked around for the slave who would wash their feet. No slave. They took off their sandals anyway and entered the room.

Jesus wanted the night to be special. It would be his last Passover meal with his friends before his death. It would be their final night together prior to his suffering.

The Lord's heart ached as he contemplated the betrayal of Judas, the denial of Peter, the desertion of his disciples, the rejection of the Jews, and his own coming death.

The future of his mission rested on the shoulders of these twelve men. Time and again he had told them that the greatest in God's Kingdom would be the least. Jesus had emphatically reminded them that he had not come to be served but to serve (Matthew 20:28).

They hadn't learned too well.

An ugly argument broke out during dinner. Luke tells us that "a dispute arose among them as to which of them was considered to be greatest" (Luke 22:24).

As the disciples fought, Jesus quietly disrobed and wrapped a servant's towel around his waist. By the door sat a pitcher filled with water; beside it was a wash basin. The Lord poured water into the basin, walked over to the disciples, knelt down, and gently washed their feet. Silence and embarrassment filled the room. The argument was over as to who would be greatest.

After Jesus had cleaned their dirty feet, he told his men, "You call me 'Teacher' and 'Lord,' and rightly so, for that is what I am. Now that I, your Lord and Teacher, have washed your feet, you also should wash one another's feet" (John 13:13, 14).

Jesus didn't tell the disciples to do "what" he did, but "as" he did. He commanded them—and us—to be servants. Following Jesus means consciously choosing to serve others, even our competitors.

Translating such lofty ideas into experience takes patience.

"Sure Dad," Ryan said, "sure I'm gonna serve the guys on the other team. And how am I supposed to do that? I wanna beat them, not help them."

"Actually, Ryan," I replied, "I don't think the Lord meant we're supposed to let our opponents beat us. He meant we're to play fairly and graciously. When we don't like a referee's call, we don't hassle him. If an opponent cheats, we're still to play by the rules. And if we can show an opponent how to improve his game, we should do so."

It's easy in the heat of battle to forget about serving the Lord and others. Anybody knows that who has ever watched, coached, or played in an athletic event. But something about the Lord enabled him to freely serve others.

Know Yourself

A "Bloom County" cartoon a while back showed the now famous penguin, Opus, looking at his reflection in a mirror. "They say I'm a penguin, eh?" he said as he gazed in the mirror. "This! This is a penguin? A rotund belly, a sway back, flat, damp feet, a more-than-generous honker—a tad lopsided and slightly mushy to the touch—and a sizable, well-cushioned tush, lumpy and mellow with age, like fine cheese. Yessir . . . whatever I am or am not, one thing remains certain: I'm almost startlingly good looking."

This strange-looking creature had no need to compare himself with others because he felt good about himself. He considered himself a winner. He liked what he saw in the mirror.

Many of us don't enjoy such an attitude; nor do our children. We aren't satisfied with our personalities, looks, possessions, athletic abilities, or intelligence. Thus, we scratch and scrape on the field of competition to prove we're okay. And we teach our children to do the same.

William Glasser in his book *Reality Therapy* noted that the two most fundamental needs of all people are the needs for security and significance.[20] We all need to feel loved and important.

Children's sports can easily become the place parents and kids turn for acceptance and importance. Parents gain vicarious significance through the accomplishments of their kids. Children feel accepted if they can score a touchdown or hit a home run.

Won't children fight to win if they believe that only by winning they will be loved by their parents and respected by their friends? Doesn't it make sense that they might cry after a loss if they believe losing brings rejection?

Like Opus, parents and children need to feel good about themselves, even if they have a rotund belly, sway back, flat, damp feet, and a big honker. Or if they lose a game.

How could Jesus freely serve his followers while they competed with one another? John 13:3b gives us the answer. John tells us the Lord knew "that He had come from God and was returning to God." That knowledge allowed Jesus to serve others by giving him absolute significance and security.

What could give more significance than knowing your origin and destiny are linked with the Creator of the universe? What could give more security than knowing your Heavenly Father accepts you? Jesus didn't have to beat his competitors in order to be a winner. He was a winner because of his relationship with God. Our problems occur when we forget that God alone can give us lasting significance and security.

Duane Thomas, a Dallas Cowboy's running back, was interviewed on television following his team's victory over Miami in Super Bowl VI. The reporter asked Thomas how it felt to win the ultimate game. Duane surprised the reporter when he asked why, if they had just played the ultimate game, two teams would play it again in one year.

Thomas had some insight. He realized that the emotional rush of winning the Super Bowl would fade. He knew the glitter of a Super Bowl ring would tarnish. He understood that yesterday's hero would soon become a forgotten footnote on the page of a history book.

Mickey Mantle fan that I am, I was touched by an article in which the great Yankee slugger described a recurring dream. Repeatedly he dreamed about standing outside a ball park and unsuccessfully trying to get in. Retired athletes like Mantle know that the glory of victory vanishes and can't be regained.

But there is a relationship which gives infinite significance and eternal security. What Christ enjoyed with his Father is offered to us. Through his death Jesus removed the guilt of our sins. Through his resurrection he offers eternal life. Those who accept Christ by trusting in him for forgiveness and eternal life enter into a relationship with God through Christ. That relationship forms the basis for all significance and security.

Like Christ, we have an intimate relationship with our Heavenly Father. And like Christ, we must wait for our Heavenly Father to exalt us at the proper time. We must wait for God to give us those victories he wants us to have.

Years after he struggled with an overly competitive spirit, Peter wrote, "Humble yourselves, therefore, under God's mighty hand, that He may lift you up in due time" (1 Peter 5:6).

When we view others only as competitors we reduce them to obstacles standing in our way of victory. We forget they are human beings with disappointments, desires, hurts, and needs.

I've seen parents, players, and coaches totally dominated by their desire to win. We must constantly remind ourselves, and our children, that there are things in life more important than winning. We must remember to draw our sense of security and significance from our relationship with God. We must try to serve our competitors through our gracious attitude and fair play.

The Lord will give us ultimate victory if we look to him. And you know what? I'm also confident he'll let us win a few along the way.

ON THE PRACTICE FIELD

1. Take some time at dinner this week to have a family discussion about the role of competition in life. Ask your children why they play sports. Discover how they feel when they win or lose.

2. Memorize Colossians 3:23, 24 as a family. Review the verse periodically, as a family, and talk about how it can be applied to life.

13

Practice

It's impossible to adequately communicate the need each of us has for parental affirmation. Jerry's story shows just how great that need is.

"Every day dad would toss me my baseball glove, pick up a ball and bat, and race me through our house," Jerry recalled. "In our backyard he'd knock me grounders. It was great! My last year in Little League I didn't make a single fielding error. Nothing got past me.

"During football season he taught me how to pass a football. When I was in high school he seldom missed a practice. Words can't express the love I had for that man. I lived for him . . . and he lived for me."

But something happened one day to change that. You sense a deep pain in Jerry's lined face as he recalls the incident.

"I remember the day of my injury," he said. "I took the snap from center and sprinted to the right. The play was a pass-run option. I decided to keep the ball. On my outside I saw a defensive end racing toward me. I cut to the inside hoping to squeeze between a linebacker and the defensive end. The instant I cut I felt my knee pop as two defenders hit my leg from opposite sides. Several teammates helped me off the field.

"After the injury things weren't the same. I lost my agility. I could still compete, but not like before.

"Dad's great dreams for my future were shattered. He couldn't accept my disability. He accused me of being lazy. He said I wasn't tough enough. He wanted me to get out there and try. But every time I cut sharply on the basketball court or football field, my knee buckled.

"I felt inadequate, rejected. I wanted my dad to give me a hug and say, 'Hey, it's okay! Do what you can and enjoy your life!' But he didn't. I realized I wasn't what he wanted in a son. I'd let him down."

Ten years passed. Jerry finished college, got married, entered his profession. Still he felt like a little boy who desperately needed a hug from his dad. Then one day the phone rang.

"I vividly remember the day he called me long distance and said: 'Son, I called to say I love you; I just want you to know I really love you,'" Jerry said. "I can't tell you the impact those three words had on my self-esteem. He was telling me I was okay, my new career was okay. Dad loved me!"

Like Jerry, each of us needs to know that our parents accept us unconditionally. We parents need to communicate our love to our children.

"Bill, that's great," you may be saying, "but what is all of this doing in a chapter on practice?"

Actually, this chapter isn't about how to plan or direct an athletic practice. It's a chapter about what parents should practice while their children sharpen their athletic skills. It's a chapter about building your child's self-esteem while helping them develop athletically.

Commitment to Affirm

In the introduction to his book, *Hide or Seek*, James Dobson describes a television interview with John McKay, the former University of Southern California football coach. At the time of the interview John's son, John Junior, played for USC. The interviewer wanted to know McKay's impression of his son's performance over the past year.

"Yes," the coach said, "I'm pleased that John had a good season last year. He does a fine job and I am proud of him. But I would be just as proud if he had never played the game."

Coach McKay made it clear that while he appreciated his son's athletic skills, his human value didn't rest on his ability to play football. Regardless of what happened on the playing field, John McKay loved and accepted his son.[21]

Like McKay, we need to affirm our children no matter how they perform on the field of competition. Our kids need parental acceptance. Jesus, our example, modeled for us the affirmation of children.

Mobbed by spectators and guarded by his disciples, Jesus took the time to welcome and bless a group of little children.

Parents were bringing their children to Jesus so he could touch them, but the disciples rebuked them. When Jesus saw this, he was indignant. He said to the parents, "Let the little children come to me, and do not hinder them, for the kingdom of God belongs to such as these." And he took the children in his arms, put his hands on them and blessed them.

The Greek word for "bless" meant "to speak well of" or "to praise someone."[22] In Old Testament times a blessing transferred a good thing from one person to another. When Isaac, under God's direction, blessed Jacob, he imparted the promise of bountiful crops, many servants, and leadership in the family (Genesis 27:27-29).

While we don't have the ability to give a blessing of such benefits, our blessings and words of affirmation can pass on valuable gifts to our children. A sense of security and destiny is one of the best gifts we can give.

Affirmation flows from love like water from a spring. To affirm our children we must consciously decide to love and accept them, no matter what. Regardless of their appearance or actions, we must love them. We might not like everything they do, but we must choose to love them anyway.

How can you demonstrate such love to your children while they are involved in sports? The answer is right under your nose.

Verbal Affirmation

Jesus opened his mouth and spoke a blessing to the children gathered around him. Years before, Abraham spoke a blessing to Isaac, Isaac uttered a blessing to Jacob, and Jacob spoke a blessing to his twelve sons and two grandchildren. As Gary Smalley and John Trent observed, "In the Scriptures, a blessing is not a blessing until it's spoken."[23]

A study of maladjusted students in a large Oklahoma high school reveals the importance of verbal affirmation.

The counselors in the school first developed close relationships with ten of the school's most troubled teenagers. Next the counselors asked the kids, "How long has it been since your parents told you they loved you?" Only one of the students could remember hearing it at all, and he didn't remember when.

In sharp contrast, students in that same school who were considered well-adjusted gave answers like: "This morning," "Last evening," and "Yesterday."[24] Solomon highlighted the importance of words fitly spoken when he wrote in Proverbs 25:11: "A word aptly spoken is like apples of gold in settings of silver."

Words of affirmation uttered at the right time show the wisdom of a jeweler who places delicate golden apples in a sterling silver setting.

Words are fantastically powerful, as Solomon would remind us: "The tongue has the power of life and death" (Proverbs 18:21a). James, the half brother of Jesus, wrote that the tongue is like a bit in a horse's mouth, a rudder on a ship, or a fire which sets a forest ablaze (James 3:3-5).

The tongue. "To the physician," writes Charles Swindoll, "it's merely a two-ounce slab of mucous membrane enclosing a complex array of muscles and nerves that enable our bodies to chew, taste, and swallow."[25] But to children, a parent's tongue is the source of acceptance or rejection. It affirms or repudiates—the power of life and death.

"But my kid can't hit or catch the ball," some of you may say. "Why should I affirm his lousy playing?"

I didn't say you should affirm lousy play. I did say you should affirm the player, no matter how good (or bad) his play.

The issue is one of focus. A wart on the face of a friend isn't pretty, but it isn't the whole face. If it's all you see, however, you may begin to think of your friend as a wart. And soon he may begin to feel like one, too.

I remember watching a Little League player strike out three times a game for half the season. He didn't hit the ball once in seven games. How'd his dad respond? He stood behind the backstop and yelled, "Good swing! Great form! Nice try!" He focused on the good.

Finally, the boy came out of his slump. He shot a ball against the center field fence. Next he hit a double; then a single. All in one game!

I've never met a child who needed to be reminded of his failures. They crave words of blessing and affirmation. They need parents to focus on the positive. No, we shouldn't ignore the bad; just concentrate on the positive.

But won't kids get arrogant if we praise them all the time?

Only if we do it in the wrong way. Arrogance grows when parents compare their child's efforts to those of another. It's never good to tell our kids they play "better than Jim, or Anne."

Yet it's imperative that we offer words of praise for our kids' positive attitudes and actions.

Cindy and I make it a habit to hold our sons, gaze into their eyes, and say, "I'll love you forever, no matter what." The first time Cindy uttered those words to our middle son, he melted.

Don't wait to bless your child with words of affirmation. Don't think: *Well, I do appreciate them, but they don't need to hear me say it.* A blessing isn't a blessing until it's spoken.

Physical Affirmation

Jesus loved children. Mark said, "And he took the children in his arms, put his hands on them and blessed them" (Mark 10:16). Jesus didn't just bend over and lecture the kids. He didn't sit on a stool and coolly instruct them. No! He gathered them into his arms. He hugged them. He laid his hands on their shoulders and heads. He made them feel loved.

Suppose you were never allowed to touch anyone, or be touched. Imagine how you would feel if the authorities placed a Touching Ban on your body. What would you feel like? Rejected. Ugly. Discarded.

That's exactly how people with leprosy felt in ancient Israel. Leprosy was considered the most loathsome of diseases. Lepers were outcasts. They had to wear a covering over their mouth and shout out a warning of their approach. The words, "Unclean, Unclean!" caused others to move away whenever a leper came near. According to Leviticus 13-14, a leper suffered such defilement that anyone who touched one immediately became unclean himself.

One day a man suffering from an advanced case of leprosy approached Jesus (Mark 1:40-42). Large areas of raw flesh, scabs, and white shining spots covered much of his body. An arm or leg may already have rotted off, leaving only a stub.

He had probably not felt the touch of a human hand or the warmth of an embrace in years, perhaps decades. He lived alone on an island of loneliness.

How did Jesus respond? He did the unthinkable. He touched the man. He felt the grotesque. He healed the leper, broke a bubble of loneliness and brought acceptance and love to that hurting soul. Mark wrote, "Filled with compassion, Jesus reached out his hand and touched the man . . ." (Mark 1:41a).

On another occasion Jesus saw the sick mother-in-law of Peter and "He touched her hand, and the fever left her . . ." (Matthew 8:15).

In Matthew 9:29 some blind men approached Jesus and the Lord "touched their eyes."

At the Mount of Transfiguration when the disciples became terrified, "Jesus came and touched them" (Matthew 17:7).

Why did Jesus so frequently reach out his hands to touch hurting people? He could have healed the leper, blind men, or Peter's mother-in-law with only a word. One likely answer is that he touched people in order to meet their immense need for love and acceptance.

Nothing communicates acceptance better than a hand on the shoulder, a pat on the back, or an embrace. Our kids need to be hugged, kissed, and lovingly touched. Sadly, many studies indicate most parents only touch their children when necessity demands. Parents usually touch their children only when they help them dress, undress, or get into a car.[26] Yet, affectionate physical contact is crucial to the emotional development of both girls and boys.[27]

I recently watched a Little League game in which one of the boys sat in his mom's lap when he wasn't playing. She repeatedly ran her hands through his hair and squeezed his shoulder. Her affection filled that child with security.

I still remember the sandpaper feel of my dad's beard and the smell of Old Spice. I recall my mom holding hands with me when we walked beside one another. Like childhood snapshots, those memories fill my mind and give me a sense of well-being.

We parents need to give our children such memories. I delight in wrestling with my three boys, and it's fun for them, too. I don't think there's anything they enjoy more than wrestling with their dad.

Several years ago I asked my youngest son how he knew I loved him. He thought for a moment and then said, "Because you wrestle with me."

Touching is simple. A gentle poke in the ribs, a ruffling of the hair, a hug, a hand on the shoulder. These affectionate acts give our kids a sense of belonging, well-being, security.

But even that's not enough. There's another form of affirmation they need.

Predictive Affirmation

Repeatedly God reminds his children of the greatness of their future. When God first spoke to Abraham he promised to give him land, many descendants, and a special heir through whom the world would be blessed (Genesis 12:1-3). Later, God promised Isaac a future to look forward to (Genesis 26:24). A generation later God appeared to Jacob in a dream and promised to give him the land upon which he slept (Genesis 28:13).

Jesus repeatedly stretched the imagination of his disciples with predictions about their future. In Matthew 19:28 he promised they would sit upon thrones judging the twelve tribes of Israel. During the last supper Jesus told them he was going to prepare dwelling places for them in his Father's house (John 14:2).

The promises didn't stop with biblical characters; God also gives us wonderful pictures for the future: " . . . when he appears, we shall be like him, for we shall see him as he is" (1 John 3:2b).

What a promise! One day all believers will instantly be transformed into the image of Jesus.

Fixing our hope on such a promise shapes our personalities and builds our futures. The more we imagine ourselves becoming like Jesus, the more we are like him. That's why John said, "Everyone who has this hope in him purifies himself, just as he is pure" (1 John 3:3).

Now, we can't make predictions like those God made of Abraham, Jacob, or Isaac. We can't speak of our children's future with the confidence John had when he spoke of a believer's destiny. But we can know our children well enough to imagine what God might accomplish through them.

We must remember that no two children are alike. Each is unique, like snowflakes. We need to know and accept those differences and allow them to shape the fabric of our dreams. As we understand the special qualities of each child we must imagine what they might some day become. And we need to share with our children what we picture them being and doing.

I know a parent whose entertaining son ties their family in knots of laughter. After one hilarious moment, I heard the boy's dad say, "Son, I can just see you someday standing before crowds in a courtroom, theater, or church. You'll be a great communicator some day!"

One young girl announced her intention to run in the Olympics some day. Did her parents correct her exaggerated hopes? No! They shared in her dream. They encouraged her to reach for the stars.

Such words of encouragement are like a lighthouse during a storm. They guide a child to the safety and warmth of sincere love and realized potential. They prevent a child from being tossed about by discouragement and aimlessness. They give a sense of significance and security.

I genuinely thank God for a mom and dad who always affirmed me with words of hope about my future. They saw more in me than others saw. They made me believe their dreams. Like a guiding star, their words kept me moving on when everything around me seemed dark.

That's why at night, when the lights are out, and the house is quiet, I hug my sons in their bed and say, "Someday, somehow, I believe God will use you to ————————————." For each son the picture is unique. It's their picture, hung in their mind, with the Lord and them at the center.

Take time to affirm your child! Imagine what they could be in the Lord, and tell them. Give them the blessing they need!

Although I only knew Arthur De Moss casually, his life left a mark on mine. As few others he modeled the balance between a drive to succeed in business and a passion to serve the Lord and his family.

As the president of a large insurance company, he rubbed shoulders with national leaders, and lovingly pointed them to Christ.

Following his death in September 1979, Nancy, a daughter, commented, "Of the ten greatest men I have ever known, this man was the greatest. He was the person who led me to the Lord, taught me to pray, taught me to believe God for great things, and convinced me through his life that I could touch the world for Christ."

She didn't praise her father's money, power, or possessions. She praised him for convincing her, through his life, that God could use her to touch the world for Christ.

I wonder . . . do you think Arthur De Moss used to dream with Nancy when she was a little girl in his arms? Did he help her imagine herself reaching others for Christ? I'm sure he did.

I hope that someday my boys give me such a tribute. Wouldn't you like your kids to speak of you that way? They may, you know, if you'll affirm them today. Go ahead! Commit to bless them with your

words, your touches, your dreams. It's an invest-
ment that will last for eternity.

NOTE: For a more exhaustive treatment of the subject found in this chapter I would recommend the book
The Blessing, by Gary Smalley & John Trent, Ph.D. I'm
indebted to them for their insights.

NOTES

1. Charles R. Swindoll, *You and Your Child* (Nashville: Thomas Nelson, 1977), pp. 18, 19.

2. Tim LaHaye, *Transformed Temperaments* (Wheaton, Ill.: Tyndale House, 1971), p. 63.

3. John G. Geier and Ken Voges, *Biblical Personal Profile Inventory* (Minneapolis: Performax Systems International, Inc., 1985), p. 21.

4. Virginia Satir, *Peoplemaking* (Palo Alto, Calif.:Science and Behavior Books, 1972), p. 64.

5. LaHaye, *Transformed Temperaments*, p. 127.

6. Bruce Cook and Howard Hendricks, *Teammates: How to Keep Building a Better Marriage* (Atlanta:Leadership Dynamics, 1987), p. 24.

7. Donald E. Sloat, *The Dangers of Growing Up in a Christian Home* (Nashville: Thomas Nelson, 1986), p. 50.

8. Geier and Voges, *Biblical Personal Profile*, p. 7.

9. Satir, *Peoplemaking*, p. 70.

10. Leon Wood, *A Survey of Israel's History* (Grand Rapids, Mich.: Zondervan, 1973), p. 92.

11. John G. Geier, *The Personal Profile System* (Minneapolis: Performax Systems International, Inc., 1979, rev. 1983).

12. Gary Smalley, *The Key to Your Child's Heart* (Waco, Tex.: Word Books, 1984), pp. 109-10.

13. Bil Gilbert, "Competition," *Sports Illustrated*, May 1988, p. 97.

14. James H. Bryan and Nancy H. Walbek, "Preaching and Practicing Generosity: Children's Actions and Reactions," *Child Development* 41 (1970): 329-53; and "The Impact of Words and Deeds Concerning Altruism upon Children," *Child Development* 41 (1970): 747-57.

15. Gilbert, "Competition," p. 97.

16. Kyle Rote, Jr., with Ronald Patterson, *Beyond the Goal* (Key Word Books, 1976), p. 76.

17. Ibid., p. 61.

18. Ibid., Introduction.

19. Alfie Kohn, "How to Succeed without Really Trying," *Psychology Today*, 1986, p. 22.

20. William Glasser, *Reality Therapy* (New York: Harper & Row, 1965), p. 9.

21. James Dobson, *Hide or Seek* (Revell, 1979), p. 13.

22. Colin Brown, *Dictionary of New Testament The-ology*, vol. 1 (Grand Rapids, Mich.:Zondervan), p. 206.

23. Gary Smalley and John Trent, *The Blessing* (Nashville:Thomas Nelson, 1986), p. 50.

24. John M. Drescher, *Seven Things Children Need* (Scottsdale, Penn.: Herald Press, 1976), p. 77.

25. Charles R. Swindoll, *Growing Strong in the Seasons of Life* (Portland, Ore.: Multnomah, 1983), p. 21.

26. Ross Campbell, *How to Really Love Your Child* (Wheaton, Ill.: Victor Books, 1987), p. 45.

27. Ibid., p. 49.

APPENDIX 1

IDENTIFYING BASIC PERSONALITY STYLES

I. IDENTIFYING AN ACTIVE-EXTROVERT

A. Is the person more concerned with:

    1. Relating well with others?

       (Cheerleader parent/Persuader child)

             OR

    2. Directing others?

       (Producer parent/Go-Getter child)

             OR

    3. Both? (See B).

B. Is the person more concerned with:

    1. Persuading others?

       (Cheerleader parent/Persuader child with some tendencies of a Producer parent/Go-Getter child).

             OR

    2. Reaching a goal—getting results?

       (A Producer parent/Go-Getter child with some tendencies of a Cheerleader parent/Persuader child).

II. IDENTIFYING A LESS ACTIVE-INTROVERT

A. Is this person more concerned with:

    1. How to accomplish results?

       (Expert parent/Specialist child)

             OR

2. The quality and importance of the assignment?
(Idealist/Thinker)
3. Both? (If both proceed to B).

B. Is the person more:
1. Tolerant and accepting of others? (Expert/Specialist with some Idealist/Thinker tendencies)
2. Analytical and critical of others? Idealist/Thinker with some Expert/Specialist tendencies).

APPENDIX 2

THE PERFORMAX PROFILE SYSTEM

The Performax Profile System (PPS) is an inventory designed to describe people's behavioral tendencies in everyday language. Developed by a psychologist, the PPS wouldn't technically be considered a personality test. It wasn't designed to reach into the depths of a person's mind as with many psychological tests. The PPS is an inventory designed to describe people's behavioral tendencies by highlighting their strengths and weaknesses.

The PPS divides people into two main categories and then subdivides those two categories into two more categories. The main groups are "active" and "less active." Other familiar terms would be "extrovert" (active) or "introvert" (less active).

Less active people adapt to their environment rather than try to change it. They focus on the "why" and "how" of things and usually feel comfortable with the "status quo."

The active category is subdivided into persons with a "dominance" or "influencing" style, and the less active category into persons with a "steadiness" or "compliance" style.

The four categories—"Dominance," "influence," "Steadiness," and "Compliance"—constitute the DiSC system. These categories are usually referred to by their first letter. "High D's" for example, tend to take charge;

the "High i" tends to be verbal; the "High S" tends to avoid conflict; the "High C" tends to be analytical.

The "i," you will notice, isn't capitalized. During the early development of the inventory, the "i" wasn't capitalized due to a printer's mistake. The developers left it that way to give a distinctive quality to the PPS system.

In this book, these descriptive titles have been changed to fit the subject matter. The high "D" is called a "Producer" parent or "Go-Getter" child. The "i" is called a "Cheerleader" parent or "Persuader" child. The "S" is called an "Expert" parent or "Specialist" child. The "C" is called an "Idealist" parent or "Thinker" child. In using the PPS, it's important to realize that each person has a primary and secondary trait. Identifying the primary trait helps understand the major characteristics of a personality. No one is just a high "D" or "C." The secondary trait rounds out the personality and aids in understanding a person's behavior. In this book we have concentrated on the primary trait.

The PPS inventory for adults and children is available through Dr. Rod Cooper for $8.00, including postage. If you would like to have a more complete understanding of your personality style and that of your child, please write to:

> Colorado Christian College
> c/o Dr. Rod Cooper
> 180 South Garrison St.
> Lakewood, Colorado 80226
> (303) 238-5826

Dr. Cooper gives seminars on personality styles as they relate to coaching, parenting, and marriage. If you are interested in hosting a seminar, please request information at the address listed above.